# Praise for Jehovah-Rapha

"We are convinced *Jehovah-Rapha* w··
multitudes. This book will be transfc
—Mark & Kathy Strandjord, Co-fou

"*Jehovah-Rapha* allures the reader wi
who changes lives."
—Kristi Graner, MA, Founding Director of Dare To Believe Ministries
and Regional Director, Bethel Sozo

"[Mary Nelson's] personal victory over sickness is a powerful testimony
of God's love and power available to all. I can hear God's still, small voice
calling me to pursue greater things in His kingdom through the Bible
stories and the testimonies in this book."
—Paul Yadao, Author, Speaker, and Lead Pastor of Destiny Ministries
International

"Mary J. Nelson wrote this great book to connect the healing hand of
God with the suffering life of humanity. Reading and meditating on these
story-based meditations and prayers will surely bring hope, healing, and
renewal of life."
—Rev. Dr. Gemechis Desta Buba, President of Leadstar College, Director of Leadstar Television, Worldwide Preacher and Teacher on Biblical
Leadership

"The Holy Spirit is all over this book! It must be put into the hands
anyone who needs healing, and it needs to be read by all who minister in
healing."
—Jim and Ramona Rickard, Founders IAHM, International Association
of Healing Ministries/Founders, RAIN—Resurrection Apostolic International Network

"Every once in a while a book comes along that you just know is going to
have a powerful and far-reaching impact. This is one of those books!
. . . As you begin the journey through these pages, get ready to encounter
Jehovah-Rapha, the God who heals."
—Leif Hetland, Founder and President of Global Mission Awareness,
Author of *Seeing Through Heaven's Eyes*

"*Jehovah-Rapha: The God Who Heals* is an extraordinary collection of
stories and meditations on healing. Mary J. Nelson has an intimate knowledge of pain and how to deal with it. This book will give you hope, healing,
and—best of all—a closer and sweeter relationship with God."
—Dr. David Clarke, Christian Psychologist, Speaker, and Author, *The Top
Ten Most Outrageous Couples of the Bible* and *I Don't Want a Divorce*

# JEHOVAH RAPHA
## the God who heals

*72 Story-Based Meditations & Prayers*

## MARY J. NELSON

**SHILOH RUN** PRESS

An Imprint of Barbour Publishing, Inc.

Published in association with the literary agency of Credo Communications, LLC, Grand Rapids, Michigan, www.credocommunications.net.

Cover Design: Greg Jackson, Thinkpen Design

Published by Shiloh Run Press, an imprint of Barbour Publishing, Inc., P.O. Box 719, Uhrichsville, Ohio 44683, www.shilohrunpress.com

*Our mission is to publish and distribute inspirational products offering exceptional value and biblical encouragement to the masses.*

Member of the
Evangelical Christian
Publishers Association

# Dedication

To Jesus, My Lord and Healer; to Hosanna! Church in Lakeville, Minnesota, where head knowledge became heart knowledge and I met Him face-to-face; and to Founding Pastor Bill Bohline whose trademark words, "We believe the Lord led you here," changed everything.

# Acknowledgments

*Jehovah-Rapha: The God Who Heals is* my fourth published book, and first in a series on the names of God. The revelation contained in these pages came from seeking God's heart through my own cancer healing journey, followed by fifteen years of healing prayer and discipleship ministry with thousands of people facing similar life-threatening diagnoses and brokenness. For making this book a reality, my deepest gratitude goes to:

Jehovah-Rapha, my God and Healer; for bringing healing to my body, forgiveness for my spirit, and freedom for my soul. All glory be to the Father, my Creator, Provider, and Protector; His Son, Jesus, my Companion and Friend; and the Holy Spirit, my Teacher, Guide, and Comforter.

My husband of thirty-nine years, Howie; for all you do to make this ministry possible. I couldn't do it without your love, prayers, support, and especially your sacrifice. I love you.

My children and grandchildren, Bryan, Kelly, Sharmi, Xavier, and Lila; you are a constant everyday reminder of God's goodness, abundant blessing, and extravagant love.

Hosanna! Prayer and Freedom, Pray for the Cure, Healing Prayer, Sozo team, and prayer team 3; for the honor and privilege of ministering alongside you in the trenches. Your deep passion for God and your heart to see the captives released, the prisoners freed, and the sick made well humble and inspire me.

Steve Hudson and the Hosanna! Israel team; for leading me in the footsteps of Jesus and for bringing His ministry to life.

Everyone whose personal quest for healing and wellness provided inspiration for the healing testimonies in this book; may your stories bring hope and encouragement to the sick and broken and remind them that nothing is impossible for God.

Finally, to my agent, Ann Byle, and Tim Beals of Credo Communications; for partnering with me to help bring God's message of hope and healing into the lives of those who need it most.

# Contents

# Before You Begin

*I have heard all about you, LORD. I am filled with*
*awe by your amazing works. In this time of our deep need,*
*help us again as you did in years gone by.*

HABAKKUK 3:2

## GALILEE, AD 29

*If I can just touch Him, I will be healed.* The thought ran
through her mind over and over as the crowds pressed in,
pushing and shoving against her as she tried to get closer to
the Healer. Reports of His power were spreading throughout
the villages. They had come from all over Judea with all kinds
of diseases and disabilities, each one hoping for a miracle.
Just yesterday she heard He had taken pity on a man with
advanced leprosy and healed him so he could return to his
family (Mark 1:40–44). Someone who had visited a crowded
home in Capernaum where the Healer was staying told about
how He healed a paralyzed man after four friends managed to
dig a hole through the roof and lower the man on a mat right
in front of Him (Mark 2:3–11). And in the village of Nain,
people said He had even raised a poor widow's son from the
dead (Luke 7:14)! Everywhere He went, the blind regained
their sight, the lame walked, the deaf could hear, lepers were
cured, and demons fled. She continued to push hard through
the crowd to reach Him. *If I can just get close enough to touch*
*Him, I know I will be healed, too.*

She risked everything to come today. A woman in her
condition shouldn't be out in public. Jewish laws forbade it.

She wasn't allowed to touch any man, especially a holy man of this stature, because she was unclean. The bleeding wouldn't stop. It had held her captive for twelve years now. The doctors couldn't help; and even if they could, she had no money left to pay them. She had given them everything she had and had tried all their remedies, but nothing worked. This man Jesus was her only hope. She tried inching closer to Him, but the crowd kept pushing her back. *If I can just touch Him.*

She pressed hard against the tangled mass of shouting, desperate people, trying to find an opening. *There! Is that Him?* She thought she caught a glimpse of His feet between the two people in front of her. Diving forward, she squeezed between them and stretched out her arm as far as she could reach, but she only caught the fringe of His robe on her fingertips. Instantly, she felt a surge of heat go through her body. She knew at once the bleeding had stopped. Amazed and elated, she sat back on her heels in stunned silence as the crowd noise grew distantly faint in the back of her mind. How long had she waited for this day? *I only touched the fringe of His robe!*

The Teacher knew immediately someone had intentionally touched Him. The touch released His healing power, and He had felt it go out from His body. He stopped and turned to ask the crowd, "Who touched My clothes?" The disciples were puzzled. With the crowd pressing against Him from all sides, how could He possibly ask if someone had touched Him? But Jesus persisted in looking for the person who had reached out to Him with such strong faith. "Who touched Me?" He asked again. The frightened woman trembled and fell at His feet. "It was me," she tearfully confessed. "I knew if I could get close enough to touch You I could be healed. I could only reach the fringe of Your robe, but You healed me!"

Jesus looked at her tenderly. "Daughter, your faith has made you well. Go in peace. You have been healed."


## Ahmednagar, India, 2008

The crowded line was long, and her daughter was growing tired. She picked up Amisha again, letting her rest in the crooks of her forearms. Amisha sighed and nestled her head against her mother's chest. At six, she was getting too big to carry, but standing and walking was difficult for Amisha. She had been born with her right leg shorter than the left and a twisted right foot that caused the sole to face inward. She limped when she walked, making it difficult to help with chores, play games, or keep up with her older brother and sister. How long before she reached someone who would pray? *If someone would just pray in the name of Jesus, Amisha will be healed.*

She had heard about Him. He was a Healer, a man who lived long ago and was raised from the dead. Christians worshipped Him. She had petitioned her own gods since Amisha was born, but they were angry and held back their blessing. Her only hope was this man Jesus. Earlier in the evening, the evangelist from the United States spoke of Jesus' power to save and heal to the huge crowd that had gathered under the stadium lights. Billboards throughout the town had encouraged them to come to the festival to learn more about Him. They came to be healed of every kind of disease and infirmity. They came because He was their only hope. There were few doctors and no money to pay them.

Most attending were "untouchables" like her, born into the lowest class of a caste system that banned and segregated them from full participation in Hindu social life. They were held captive to a life of discrimination, poverty, and often unrestrained violence—with no hope of escape. But this evangelist had given her hope. He said Jesus loved her. In His Kingdom, everyone was equal. Rich or poor, untouchable or not, His followers all shared the same inheritance and the same eternal future. The evangelist said Jesus could meet her every need. He could heal her and her household of sin and disease. With Him, all things were possible.

She had stood when the evangelist invited the crowd to receive Jesus as her Lord and Savior. Her heart leapt when he invited the crowd to come forward for healing prayer in Jesus' name. And now, she waited in the crowded line with everyone else who wanted to lift up their petitions and receive from God through one of the prayer ministers lined up behind the barrier. She desperately wanted Jesus to heal her little Amisha. Life would be difficult enough for someone like her, but without support, a crippled child was destined to a life of scavenging in the streets or much worse. *If someone would just pray in the name of Jesus, Amisha will be healed.*

Finally, a man signaled her to come with him. With Amisha's arms clinging tightly around her neck, she quickly followed him, pushing her way through the crowd as he led her to one of the prayer ministers. The young woman greeted her with a gentle smile and asked a question, but she couldn't understand the English words. Her eyes searched around for the man who led her through the crowd. She hoped he could translate, but he was gone, so she simply nodded toward the child who still rested in her arms. The prayer minister raised one hand to the heavens and laid the other on the child's leg and began to pray, *"Yeh Pavitra Aatmaa."* Come, Holy Spirit. The rest of the prayer was in English, so she didn't understand all the words. When it was over, the young woman looked up and smiled at her again. By this time, Amisha was squirming to be let down, so she lowered her to her feet. For a moment, the child looked puzzled. Amisha took a few tentative steps forward and looked back at her with a broad grin on her face. To her astonishment, Amisha's legs were even and her foot was straight. Praise Jesus, Amisha was healed!

---

A bleeding woman and a crippled child separated only by time, each desperate for hope and seeking mercy from the Lord who heals. Two thousand years ago, Jesus came to restore what the enemy stole in the garden, to set things right and initiate His Kingdom on earth (Matthew 12:28; Luke 4:18–20). He came to give life in all its fullness, to comfort the brokenhearted, and to set the captives free (John 10:10; Isaiah 61:1). He preached the good news of His arrival everywhere He went. *The Kingdom of God is near!* He wanted His followers to understand that His Kingdom is not just a place we may hope to experience in the future, but a realm of power making all things possible today. His Kingdom has started and will continue until it is finally finished on that day when He returns (Philippians 1:6). In this secret place under God's divine rule and reign, there is love, goodness, peace, joy, healing, and abundant life. In this secret place, no evil will conquer you (Psalm 91:9–10).

Yes, Jesus is still with us, and the good news hasn't changed. He never changes. We change. For some reason, we forget. And in our forgetfulness, perhaps we stop believing. We take our eyes off the Creator and focus instead on His creation. We become children of the world instead of children of the Kingdom. He blessed us with intelligence and free will, and we grow comfortable and dependent on a world of things we can touch, see, hear, and control. We forget about the secret place of things unseen. We stop believing that He is the Healer and His power is unlimited. Nothing is impossible for Him. We forget that Jesus preached salvation by actually saving, healing, and delivering people.

The good news of the Gospel is what Jesus did, not just what He said (Acts 10:37–38). He combined both preaching and healing and gave His disciples the power and authority to do the same in His name (Luke 9:1–2; 10:8–9). Then He told all of us to go into the world and preach the good news to everyone, everywhere. He said signs and wonders will accompany those who believe, and they will be able to place their hands on the sick and heal them (Mark 16:15–18). Through the ministry of Peter and Paul, He further demonstrated that healing and miracles were a central and vital part of the early church and His message to the world (Acts 4:29–30; 5:16; Romans 15:18–19).

He is the same today as He was two thousand years ago and before the world began. He is the same yesterday, today, and forever (Hebrews 13:8). He is not just able to heal today. He is willing. Through His death and resurrection, He provided the full measure of grace to restore *all* things (Colossians 1:20). He longs to give His children all the blessings of redemption, including physical healing. He always heals those who seek Him. The healing can come supernaturally. Often, He allows His creation to co-labor with Him in the healing process through individual prayer, doctors who provide treatments, or prayer ministers who lay hands on the sick and pray. When physical healing doesn't come, the greatest miracle of all is that He *always* heals eternally. Whatever the situation, He is still the Lord who heals.

In this book you will find compelling teaching on the healing promises of scripture, healing prayers, and powerful Kingdom stories that will guide you in your quest for healing. My hope is that through this journey, you will come to desire God more than life itself. I pray that His love will overwhelm you and you will be lost in His presence. In this deep place of intimacy with the Savior, may He release His healing power. I pray you will be filled with awe by the amazing things He has done. In this time of your deep need, may He help you again as He has in years gone by. May He show you His power to save and heal.

# Good News!

*Jesus traveled throughout the region of Galilee, teaching in
the synagogues and announcing the Good News about the Kingdom.
And he healed every kind of disease and illness.*
MATTHEW 4:23

From humble beginnings and after years of obscurity, at age thirty Jesus launched His public ministry with powerful teaching and preaching. He had good news to share—news about the Kingdom of God! For centuries, the people waited for the Anointed One who would rescue them from their Roman oppressors and establish a new Kingdom on earth. More than three hundred prophecies in the ancient scriptures foretold His coming. His cousin John the Baptist came ahead of Him to prepare the way and to tell the people how to find salvation through the forgiveness of sin (Luke 3:4–6). Finally, their long-awaited Messiah had come!

With Capernaum as His home base, Jesus traveled throughout Galilee teaching in the synagogues and preaching everywhere the good news about the Kingdom. News about Him spread far beyond the borders of Galilee. Enormous crowds gathered to hear Him preach. The people were hungry for His message of hope and salvation. People came from the Ten Towns, Jerusalem, from all over Judea, and from east of the Jordan River. Whatever their illness or pain, from the lame and epileptic to the demonically possessed, He healed them. Soon the sick were coming to be healed from as far away as Syria. No problem was too great or too small for Him. He healed them *all*.

As they watched Him heal the sick and set the captives

free, they knew His teaching was true. They witnessed proof of His power and love for them. This man was indeed sent from God! He had authority over sickness and disease—complete authority over heaven and earth (Matthew 28:18). He healed them all because it's God's nature to heal. It always has been and always will be, because our God never changes (Malachi 3:6). Jesus said anyone who has seen Him has seen the Father (John 14:9). When Jesus healed the sick, His actions reflected the Father's heart.

Today, imagine *you* stand in the crowd. You eagerly wait to hear His voice. You hunger for His message of hope. Desperately, you seek His healing touch. His eyes search the multitude and lock onto yours, slowly penetrating the depths of your soul. You know at once your Savior has come. He knows everything about you. He knows your name. He knows your every need. He knows the deepest desires of your heart. And He still has authority over sickness and disease. He has the same power and desire to heal today as He did two thousand years ago when He traveled through Galilee preaching the good news. At last, the Kingdom is here!

## Prayer

*Lord, long ago Your prophets said You would come to save me. Your prophet Isaiah said, "The people who walk in darkness will see a great light. For those who live in a land of deep darkness, a light will shine" (Isaiah 9:2). Lord, I don't want to walk in darkness anymore. I want to turn from my sin and turn to the Light (Matthew 4:17). I turn my life over to Your direction and control. Thank You, Lord, for sending Your Son to redeem me! My Messiah has come! My Lord and Savior—my King!*

*Lord, I lift up the words You taught us to pray. "Your kingdom come, your will be done, on earth as it is in heaven" (Matthew 6:10 NIV). When I pray these words, I'm praying that Your perfect purpose will be accomplished in this world as in the next. Lord, in heaven there is no illness or pain. Sickness and disease were never Your plan for me. They came into the earth through the sin of one man. Two thousand years ago, heaven touched earth in the form of another man. He healed the sick and set the captives free. Jesus, my King! You live in me. You reign in me. I believe in Your power and desire to heal me today, just as You healed people of every kind of sickness and disease when Your ministry first began. I love You, Lord. Thank You for sending Your Kingdom to earth.*

# I Am Willing

*Large crowds followed Jesus as he came down the mountainside.*
*Suddenly, a man with leprosy approached him and knelt before him.*
*"Lord," the man said, "if you are willing, you can heal me and make me*
*clean." Jesus reached out and touched him. "I am willing," he said.*
*"Be healed!" And instantly the leprosy disappeared.*

MATTHEW 8:1–3

The man bowed low before the Healer, covering his face with his tattered coat. He had long ago been banished from his home to live outside the city with others suffering the same affliction. Exile was his destiny until he was cured, no longer contagious, or until he simply died. Coming out to meet the Healer brought great risk. As a leper, he was declared by Jewish law to be unclean and was forbidden from mingling with the public or participating in any religious activities. He looked around nervously, alert for the law keepers and those who often threw rocks to keep people like him at a safe distance.

By now, the disease was advanced. It had destroyed his nerve endings, leaving unrecognizable clumps of damaged tissue where his toes, fingers, and nose once had been. In spite of his repulsive appearance, and even though his skin was covered in lesions, the Healer reached out and touched him. He had not felt the touch of a human hand in so long. The touch alone held so much love it would have satisfied him. At that same moment, the lesions instantly disappeared, and his skin was restored as a curious power gently flowed through his body.

Amazed, the man made his way to the priest who would

examine him and confirm his healing so he could be restored to his community. Only a few moments before, he had come to Jesus broken and needy. He had knelt before Him, worshipping in humble adoration of His lordship. When he said "if You want to," he acknowledged Jesus' sovereignty over all things on heaven and earth. When he said "You can make me well again," he demonstrated his faith. Even though his disease was seriously advanced, he still believed Jesus could heal him. And Jesus did. In the process, Jesus showed him that his real value was on the inside, not the outside. Jesus loved him and honored his deep reverence and submissiveness before the King.

You, too, may be deformed or diseased, but you are still valuable to God. You are still worthy of His healing touch. A healthy body is a reflection of His goodness and abundant love for you. In fact, He planned for you to live a long and satisfying life (Psalm 91:16). He promised to be your God who would care for you throughout your lifetime—until your hair is white with age (Isaiah 46:4). In the oldest of the psalms, Moses notes in his prayer that God gives us a life span of seventy to eighty years (Psalm 90:10). Moses himself lived a long and full life of 120 years and died strong as ever, without illness, and with clear eyesight (Deuteronomy 34:7). Jesus showed His heart for you and for all when He told the leper He *wanted* to heal him. Worship Him now in holy fear and awe. Humbly seek Him for your healing. Hear His gentle voice say, "I am willing."

# Prayer

*Father, like the leper in this story, I fall down on my knees and worship You. I come broken and desperately needing Your healing power. I am fully dependent on You for my every breath and my very existence (Acts 17:28). Without You, I am nothing. You are my God and my King, my Creator, Sustainer, and Redeemer! I love You with all my heart, all my soul, all my mind, and all my strength (Mark 12:30). I praise You and thank You for who You are and all You have done for me. I bless You, Lord, and give You all the glory!*

*Lord, You are sovereign over my life. You are sovereign over this affliction. You are sovereign over all the doctors who have cared for me and all the drugs and treatments they have used to bring healing to my body. You alone have the power to heal me by whatever method You choose—supernaturally, medically, eternally. Lord, I know You love me, and I am made worthy by Your blood. I believe You want to heal me. I believe it is Your nature to heal. I believe nothing is too hard for You. You can make me well again. Touch me, Lord! Let me hear the words, "I am willing." Let me hear the words, "Be healed."*

# The God of Compassion

*Jesus saw the huge crowd as he stepped from the boat,*
*and he had compassion on them and healed their sick.*
MATTHEW 14:14

Jesus went off by boat to a remote area to be alone and grieve. He had just learned of His cousin's fate. John, who had paved the way for Him, was dead—beheaded at the whim of a young girl doing her mother's evil bidding. Herod imprisoned John for declaring that it was illegal for Herod to marry his brother's wife, Herodias. He would have executed him, but he feared a riot. His wife handled the problem for him when she urged her daughter to demand John's head on a platter as a reward for her pleasing dance performance.

When the people heard where Jesus was going, they followed Him. Instead of finding solitude when He stepped off the boat, He found a vast crowd of needy people from many villages waiting for Him. Cripples, lepers, the blind and deaf, and hordes of sick people all shouted, "Teacher, touch me! Make me well again!" as they pushed and shoved toward Him, clamoring for His attention. He didn't send them away. In spite of His own deep grief, He had compassion on them and healed all who were sick (Matthew 14:1–14).

Jesus didn't heal the vast crowds that came to Him just to prove He was sent from heaven. He preached salvation by healing and saving people because He had deep compassion for the sick and oppressed. He could see they were like sheep without a shepherd. Their needs were so great, and they didn't know where to go for help (Matthew 9:36). Like lost sheep, they wandered aimlessly though life, sick and broken, alone and hopeless, desperate for a Shepherd who would come to lead and guide them. They longed for someone to comfort and protect them. They desperately needed someone to love and heal them.

God has always been kind and merciful to His creation (Psalm 145:8–10). He has shown His unfailing love and compassion throughout the ages (Psalm 25:6). His compassion compelled Him to restore Israel even though the people repeatedly failed to follow His commandments and heed His warnings to turn from their sin (Zechariah 10:6). Compassion overflowed in His heart when He raised the only son of a widow from the dead (Luke 7:13–15). Compassion moved Him to pity a begging man and heal him from leprosy (Mark 1:41).

Today you may feel lost, but your Shepherd never stops looking for you. You may feel alone and misunderstood, but He is no stranger to your pain. He also endured much. He was mocked, spat on, whipped, and beaten beyond recognition. Nails pierced His hands and feet so you could live in victory. He suffered and died to prove His love for you. He is like a father to His children, tender and compassionate to those who fear Him (Psalm 103:13). Wait expectantly for Him to pour out His grace and mercy. Wait expectantly for His healing touch. Wait and know that in *all* things He is good. He is the God of compassion.

# Prayer

*Lord, Your Word says that You bless those who wait for Your help (Isaiah 30:18). Today, I wait. I wait for You to step off the boat and into the crowd. I wait for You to come so You can show me Your love and compassion! My needs are great and You are my only hope. You are the only One who can help me and the only One worthy of my praise. In one amazing act of love, You conquered death and disease forever. You overcame the world and all its troubles! You conquered all my afflictions. Thank You, Father, for the gift of Your Son. He died so I can live. My human mind simply can't comprehend a love so deep.*

*You are my Shepherd, Lord. I have wandered too long in this valley of pain and sickness. Too long have I lived in this shadow of death. Have compassion on me, Lord! Gather me in Your arms and carry me to safety! Lead me and guide me. Show me Your pathway to health and restoration. Comfort and protect me. Draw me close to Your heart and overwhelm me with Your love. Reveal Yourself, Lord. Pour out Your Spirit and make Your powerful presence known to me. Lord, have mercy. Touch me and heal me!*

# The Perfect Plan

*Yet it was our weaknesses he carried; it was our sorrows that
weighed him down. And we thought his troubles were a punishment
from God, a punishment for his own sins! But he was pierced for our
rebellion, crushed for our sins. He was beaten so we could be whole.
He was whipped so we could be healed.*

Isaiah 53:4–5

"Are You the king of the Jews?" the governor demanded.
"You have said so," Jesus replied. But when confronted by
His accusers, the chief priests and elders, Jesus said nothing.
Baffled by His silence, the governor asked, "Don't You hear the
testimony they are bringing against You?" Again, Jesus made
no reply, not to a single charge (Matthew 27:11–14). After
Pilate sentenced Him to death by crucifixion, the soldiers
stripped Him, flogged Him with a lead-tipped whip, twisted
together a crown of sharp thorns and set it on His head,
and put a staff in His right hand. Not once did He defend
Himself. He silently endured as they spit on Him, beat Him
on the head with a stick, and dropped to their knees in mock
worship, hailing Him as the "King of the Jews" (Matthew
27:26–30; Mark 15:15–19). He went willingly to the cross—
beaten, bloodied, and so disfigured that no one even knew
He was a person (Isaiah 52:14). Upon this Suffering Servant
God laid the guilt and sins of the entire world (Isaiah 53:6).

When God revealed His secret plan to the prophet
Isaiah, He pulled back the curtain of time. The people of
Israel never dreamed that God would save them through a
Suffering Servant rather than a mighty king. But God always
works opposite of worldly thinking. He used a slave to save

them from a great famine and a murderer to lead them out of bondage to the Promised Land (Genesis 39; Exodus 3). He chose a farmer to deliver them from the Midianites and a shepherd boy to be their greatest king (Judges 6:11–14; 1 Samuel 16). Instead of sending a strong warrior to overthrow their Roman oppressors, He sent a gentle carpenter to save the world. Jesus demonstrated His strength through humility and obedience to His mission.

Isaiah knew this unlikely King would come to save you. He has already purchased your healing with His blood. When they whipped Him, you were healed. When He dragged the cross up the hill to Calvary, He carried the weight of your sickness on His back (1 Peter 2:24). When they nailed Him to the cross, He defeated your disease and carried it with Him to the grave. When He arose in triumph, His perfect plan was revealed to the entire world.

# Prayer

*Lord, when I think of all You have done for me, I can scarcely breathe. I fall to my knees in humble adoration, overwhelmed with gratefulness for Your obedience to Your earthly mission. Father, because You loved me so much, You orchestrated the perfect plan to redeem me from the sin that had come into the world through one man (Romans 5:12). Your plan must seem so foolish to the philosophers, the scholars, and the world's brilliant thinkers. But I know You work opposite of worldly thinking. I know Your plan is far wiser than the wisest of human plans, and Your weakness is far stronger than the greatest of human strength (1 Corinthians 1:18–25).*

*Lord, You sent an unlikely King to save the world. You sent Your only Son, a gentle carpenter. When He walked the earth as a man, He healed the sick, fulfilling the words of the prophet Isaiah, who said, "He took our sicknesses and removed our diseases" (Matthew 8:17). Jesus, my Savior! God laid upon You the sins of the world. He laid upon You the weight of my sickness. You were beaten, and I found peace. You were whipped, and I was healed. You bled and died for me. Thank You for purchasing my healing with Your blood.*

# In His Name

*"Through faith in the name of Jesus, this man was healed—
and you know how crippled he was before. Faith in
Jesus' name has healed him before your very eyes."*
ACTS 3:16

It was nearly time for three o'clock worship. The man watched as Peter and John approached the Beautiful Gate to enter the temple. Lame from birth, he knew it was a praiseworthy act in the Jewish culture to give money to a crippled beggar like him. Each day, he shrewdly placed himself where he could be seen by the most people and take advantage of their pious generosity. When Peter and John reached the temple entrance, he asked them for money, eagerly expecting the usual coins. But Peter surprised him with a life-changing gift. He said, "I don't have any money for you. But I'll give you what I have. In the name of Jesus Christ of Nazareth, get up and walk!" To the man's amazement, his feet and ankle bones were immediately healed.

Praising God and leaping for joy, he followed Peter and John into the temple as the crowd stood in awe of what they had just witnessed. Peter was quick to give Jesus the glory for the healing: "Through faith in the name of Jesus, this man was healed—and you know how crippled he was before. Faith in Jesus' name has healed him before your very eyes." He used the opportunity to preach to them about Jesus the Messiah, the One whom God appointed long ago to die for their sin (Acts 3:1–20).

In that culture, a man's name represented his character and stood for his authority and power. When Peter said, "*In the name of Jesus Christ* get up and walk," he was saying "by the authority of Jesus Christ." The *name* of Jesus healed this man—faith in His *name* caused this healing to occur before the crowd's very eyes. He was healed through the power of the Holy Spirit, not through any power of Peter's. Peter was only an obedient vessel acting under the authority Jesus gave to him, just as Jesus acted under the authority of His Father (Matthew 28:18–19; Luke 24:47).

As a believer, you have the same authority as Peter to pray for healing in Jesus' name (Mark 16:17–18). But we must be careful not to take His name lightly or use it with the wrong heart. Simon the Sorcerer made this mistake when he offered money to buy the power of God after watching Peter and John lay hands on the believers to receive the Holy Spirit. His heart was unclean before God, and the apostles admonished him to turn from his wickedness (Acts 8:9–24). Jesus warned that not everyone who prophesies, casts out demons, or performs miracles in His name does so by His authority. It is possible to look religious and say the right words with the wrong motives (Matthew 7:21–23).

The name of Jesus is holy. It should be honored and spoken with deep humility, a pure heart, and the reverence due our Lord and Savior. It's not the sound of His name that gives your prayers their power. It's the Holy Spirit within you. It's Jesus Christ Himself. Pray in His name by faith. Pray in His name and be healed.

# Prayer

*Lord, thank You for Your grace, Your wisdom, Your goodness, and Your healing power! This man begged only for money, but You gave him something much better. You gave him the use of his legs so he would never have to beg again. The power and authority of Your name changed his life! How often, Lord, do I ask for something small when You want to give me something so much bigger? You have so much more in store for me! You want to give me a whole new life in You. When I pray, You might not always give me what I want, but I know You will always give me exactly what I need. Forgive me for the times I don't trust You to know what's best for me.*

*Lord, You have complete authority over heaven and earth (John 3:35). I know You gave Your apostles authority to heal disease and cast out demons (Luke 9:1). Thank You for giving me that same authority! Lord, please increase my faith in the power of Your name. Reveal any impure motives that I need to repent so I can come before You with a pure heart! Please give me wisdom and understanding so that I might grow in my knowledge of the authority I have in You as a believer. Help me truly grasp that the Holy Spirit who dwells within me is the same mighty power that raised You from the dead and seated You in the place of honor at the Father's right hand. In the name of Jesus Christ and by His authority, I release healing over my body!*

## Jehovah-Rapha: Sanjay's Story

*Yeshu, Yeshu, Yeshu.* Slowly and carefully, Sanjay repeated the Marathi word for Jesus, trying hard to mimic the sounds as he listened to each syllable. His eyes darted around the room as if the sights and sounds overloaded his senses.

Sanjay had been born deaf. His mother noticed he didn't react to loud noises or respond to their voices when he was just an infant. Her sister's children began talking at about nine months and were putting words into sentences by two years. Sanjay said nothing. Now, at six years old, he still gazed at them with deep, soulful brown eyes, oblivious to the enveloping sounds of honking horns, moving traffic, construction, and neighborhood chatter. Sanjay played alone, content in his silent world. Until today.

Sanjay's father worried about him. He was a good father. Unlike most in India, he had an education and a decent job at the local university. *Will Sanjay ever be so blessed?* he wondered. The doctor had said he would never hear or speak. There were no special schools for the deaf even remotely close to their community, and it was too expensive to send him away. Without an education, there was no way for a deaf and mute child to make a living when he grew up. *What will happen when I can't care for him anymore?*

But a coworker at the university had taken a special interest in Sanjay. The man was a Christian. "Bring Sanjay to my church and let the elders pray for him in Yeshu's name to be healed," he urged. As a Hindu, Sanjay's father didn't hold much hope in another god who claimed to be a healer. But his friend was insistent. He would be interpreting this weekend for a guest pastor from the United States, and a group of prayer ministers would be with him to minister to the sick. "Yeshu heals! Bring Sanjay to the church and he will be healed!" his friend said. This time, Sanjay's father agreed.

He arose early with Sanjay that morning and followed his friend's directions to the church. All night long, the thought of his little Sanjay hearing and speaking had filled his mind as he drifted in and out of sleep. *How different his future would be! Is such a thing within the realm of possibility? Could this friend's Jesus really heal my son? Could He open the ears of the deaf and bring forth words from the mute?* By morning, he had allowed himself to hope. He began to believe Yeshu could do what the doctors said was impossible and what his own gods couldn't do.

They arrived at the church during a time of worship and singing, so only a few noticed their arrival. Everyone in the church had their arms raised up in worship as they jumped and shouted their praises to Jesus to the steady beat of the drum. The church was small and the crowd was large, but he found a place to sit on the floor near the back. Sanjay rested quietly on his lap, completely unaware of the sounds of joy that filled the room.

He looked for his friend but couldn't see him until the worship ended. As people were taking their seats, he watched him walk to the front to introduce the pastor. The pastor gave his message in English while his friend translated in Marathi. Some of the words he had heard before. "God loves us," "He is our heavenly Daddy," and "He has a perfect plan for our lives." *Even Sanjay?*

The world Daddy God created fell into sin, but He never stopped loving us. He loved us so much He sent His Son, Yeshu, to make us right with Him again. He didn't send His Son to condemn the world but to save it. Yeshu went around preaching the good news of salvation by doing good things and healing all who had fallen to the power of evil. He died a criminal's death, but He rose again and rules forever with fairness and justice. At the cross, He conquered sin, evil powers, and earthly disease. The same power that conquered the grave and rescued the earth lives in those who believe, the preacher said. He is the hope of all the world. *Is there hope for Sanjay?*

After the message, the pastor prayed fervently and invited people to stand for ministry time. He stood, and when a man approached him and asked if he could pray for Sanjay, he quickly agreed. In broken English, he told the man that Sanjay couldn't hear or speak. The man prayed, but nothing seemed to be happening. Sanjay grew restless, so he sat on the floor cradling the boy in his arms, weeping and praying over him for quite some time before his friend and some other prayer ministers surrounded Sanjay and joined the man in praying.

Sanjay's father hovered over the group who was praying over his son. *Yeshu, Yeshu, heal my Sanjay! Open his ears! Let him speak!* Suddenly, Sanjay held his hands over his ears and began rocking back and forth in the man's lap. He reached down for his son as Sanjay grabbed his arm frantically. Their eyes locked, and he could tell by the expression on his son's face that something extraordinary had just happened. Sanjay's mouth began moving as if to mimic the sounds he was suddenly hearing. A small sound came forth, barely audible. Then another. Finally, a syllable. Another syllable. *Yeshu.* Sanjay repeated the word over and over. *Yeshu, Yeshu, Yeshu.* Tearfully, Sanjay's father looked up at his friend. "Yeshu healed my son. I will trust in Him."

# His Tender Mercies

*He forgives all my sins and heals all my diseases.*
PSALM 103:3

King David was one of the greatest men in the Old Testament, well known as a shepherd, giant-killer, poet, mighty warrior, and ancestor of Jesus. But he was also an adulterer and murderer.

One spring afternoon while he was strolling on the roof of the palace, he spotted the beautiful Bathsheba bathing in a pool. Even though she was married to Uriah the Hittite, a loyal warrior in King David's army, he sent for her and she became pregnant. To cover his indiscretion, David summoned Uriah from the battlefield and tried to cajole him into spending the evening with his wife. When his plan failed, David sent Uriah to the front lines where the battle was fiercest. Sure enough, Uriah was killed and David took Bathsheba as his own wife.

Needless to say, the Lord was displeased and communicated His anger through the prophet Nathan, in addition to the consequences for David's actions (2 Samuel 11–12). But David was quick to confess his sin, and his repentance was genuine. God forgave him and showed him mercy and even referred to him as a "man after my own heart" (Acts 13:22). David never took God's forgiveness lightly or His blessing for granted.

In Psalm 103, David helps us focus on God's blessings and what He does for us. His tender mercies reveal how much He loves you and wants the best for you. David's list is powerful:

- He forgives all your sins.
- He heals all your diseases.
- He redeems your life from destruction.
- He crowns you with love and tender mercies.
- He satisfies your desires with good things so that your youth is renewed like the eagle's.
- He executes righteousness and judgment for you against oppression and sets you free.
- He makes known His ways to you.
- He gives you His grace and mercy in times of need.

David wrote many of the psalms during the years he was hiding in caves and running for his life from a jealous King Saul. He learned to praise and thank God even while his enemies pursued him relentlessly. Can you thank God for His tender mercies no matter how difficult your situation or how long it may take for healing to come? When answers to your prayers don't seem to be manifesting in the physical realm, you may start doubting His mercies. You may begin to wonder if He is withholding your healing because He is punishing you or because you are unworthy of His grace. You may start viewing God as a judge and lawgiver instead of a compassionate lover and a kind and patient caregiver.

The truth is, all of us are unworthy in our own humanness. Jesus died to make us worthy. He went to the cross to redeem the world to Himself. Because He loves us so much, His tender mercies start afresh every day and never come to an end (Lamentations 3:23). Great is His faithfulness! Day after day, your past doesn't matter because He wiped your record clean. You are worthy in His sight. You are worthy to receive His tender mercies. You are worthy to receive your healing. Never forget the good things He does for you. Praise Him with a whole heart. He heals *all* your diseases!

# Prayer

*Father, thank You that Your tender mercies start afresh every day! I pray You would etch David's list permanently on my heart so I will never forget all the ways You care for me. Please forgive me for the times I doubt Your mercies and Your infinite love for me. Thank You for redeeming my life from destruction and crowning me with Your loving kindness. I stand before You, righteous and worthy of Your love through the gift of Your Son. Thank You for giving me Your grace and mercy in my time of need.*

*I pray You would flood my heart with light so I can grow in my knowledge of You and the wonderful inheritance I have in Jesus. I know all the good things in my life come directly from Your loving hands (James 1:17). I'm so sorry for the times I've blamed You for things that have happened that are completely against Your nature or accused You of withholding Your love and Your blessings. You are God and You are good! In all things, You are good, even when I don't understand Your ways. All Your blessings, all Your tender mercies, and all Your compassion are mine in Jesus Christ. In Him, I am healed of all my diseases. In Him, I am free.*

# His Word Brings Life

*My son, pay attention to what I say; turn your ear to my words.*
*Do not let them out of your sight, keep them within your heart;*
*for they are life to those who find them and health to one's whole body.*

PROVERBS 4:20–22 NIV

King Solomon was the third king of Israel, the son of David and Bathsheba. Early in his reign, God appeared to him in a dream and told him to ask for anything and He would provide it. Solomon requested an understanding mind so he could govern well and know the difference between right and wrong. The Lord was so pleased with his unselfish request that He made him the wisest man who would ever live and blessed him with great wealth (1 Kings 3:5–12). He reigned forty years and wrote Ecclesiastes, Song of Songs, and most of the book of Proverbs.

In Proverbs 4:20–22, King Solomon reveals the secret to life and radiant health. In this verse, "health" means "medicine" in the Hebrew. You can find this perfect medicine in the pages of your Bible, the inspired Word of God (2 Timothy 3:16–17). Through the Holy Spirit, God revealed Himself and His plan to King Solomon and other believers who wrote down His message from their own historical and cultural contexts. They wrote what He inspired them to write, so when you study scripture, you can make it your standard for testing everything else that claims to be true.

His Word is sweet to your taste—sweeter than honey (Psalm 119:97–105). As you savor each word, you'll discover more than a collection of God-breathed words written on the pages of your Bible. The Word was God and was with

God before the world began. He created everything there is. And then the Word became human and lived on earth among us (John 1:1–14). The Word is Jesus, and He meets every human need. God sent Him out to heal you and save you from destruction (Psalm 107:20).

When you read His Word and believe by faith that His promises are true for you personally, His supernatural power can come into your situation and override your natural circumstances. Having faith is a process, and God will never condemn you for not having enough. Faith starts by choosing to agree with His Word, whether or not it lines up with your physical circumstances or experiences (Mark 11:22–24).

Just as you would build up your physical body through exercise, you can build up your faith by feeding your spirit regularly, feasting your eyes daily on His promises, reading aloud the scripture that applies to your situation, and thanking Him from a grateful heart (Hebrews 11:1). In doing so, you are calling things that are not as though they were (Romans 4:17). You begin to see yourself as God sees you, and your faith can make you well (Mark 5:34).

Every minute you spend feasting on the Word is the same as spending time at the feet of your Savior. And every minute you spend in the presence of Jesus brings you one step closer to the heart of the Father and one step closer to His healing touch. Never lose sight of Him. His words are living power and stand the test of time (Isaiah 40:8; Hebrews 4:12). Let His sacred medicine penetrate deep within your heart and bring radiant health to your body!

# Prayer

*Lord, forgive me when I wonder if the Bible is still true and if Your Word has the power to heal. I know I don't always follow Your teaching perfectly and some of it perplexes me. It doesn't mean Your Word isn't truth. It simply means we all sin and fall short of Your glorious standard (Romans 3:23). This is no surprise to You. That's exactly the reason You gave us a Savior. Lord, I'm amazed by a love so great that Your Word became flesh and lived on earth among us. Through Jesus, You pour out Your blessings and Your unfailing love and faithfulness (John 1:16–17). Thank You for sending Your Son to be the perfect teacher, the perfect example, and the perfect sacrifice.*

*Lord, thank You for Your Word revealed in scripture. Every word is truth. Every word is God-breathed. Your Word stands the test of time. Please help me not to doubt, especially when Your Word conflicts with my circumstances. Your Word is sweet, and I want to taste your goodness and mercy. I desperately want to discover the meaning of Your scripture. When I feast on Your Word, I know I am spending time in the presence of Jesus. Help me never to lose sight of You. May Your Word be a lamp for my feet and a light for my path. Every day, draw me to the scriptures that speak Your truth to me. Draw me to words that comfort me, encourage me, and testify to Your healing power. Let Your Word become medicine, penetrating deep within my heart and bringing life and radiant health to my body.*

# Help Me Not to Doubt!

*"Have mercy on us and help us, if you can." "What do you mean, 'If I can'?"*
*Jesus asked. "Anything is possible if a person believes." The father instantly*
*cried out, "I do believe, but help me overcome my unbelief!"*

MARK 9:22–24

The man stood on the crowd's fringe at the foot of the mountain. Discouraged, he listened as the disciples and religious leaders argued over his son. He had heard about this man Jesus and the healing miracles He and His disciples had performed. He brought his son today because he thought they might be able to help him, too. Ever since he was a little boy, he had been possessed by an evil spirit that rendered him deaf and mute. The spirit threw him into violent convulsions, making him foam at the mouth and grind his teeth. They couldn't leave him unattended because the spirit often threw him into fire or water, trying to kill him. The father came with hope, but now he wondered if all he had heard were just exaggerated stories.

With his hands still resting on his son's shoulders, he looked up in awe as Jesus approached the crowd and asked about the arguing. Boldly the father explained, "I asked Your disciples to heal my son, but they couldn't do it." Troubled, Jesus asked him to bring the boy to Him. But when the evil spirit saw Jesus, it threw the boy into more convulsions. "Have mercy on us and help us. Do something if You can!" cried the father. When Jesus challenged the man's faith in His ability to heal the boy, he instantly replied, "I do believe, but help me overcome my doubt!" Immediately, Jesus cast out the spirit of deafness and muteness and the boy was healed (Mark 9:14–29; Matthew 17:14–20).

When the disciples asked Him why they couldn't heal the boy, Jesus said, "This kind can be cast out only by prayer" (Mark 9:29). In Matthew's account of the same story, Jesus told them they didn't have enough faith to heal him (Matthew 17:20). Their inability to heal the boy was likely due to their own unbelief, not the doubt of the boy's father. Jesus was teaching them that prayer and faith are interrelated. The act of praying unlocks faith. Faith is sustained only through a process of daily renewal and communication with God. Jesus modeled this often when He went up on the mountainside to pray and be alone with His Father (Matthew 14:23).

The boy's father showed faith simply by bringing his son to be healed. Jesus didn't condemn him for doubting, and He won't condemn you. The father knew that faith wasn't something he could conjure up in his own power, but he could ask Jesus for more. Jesus knew how desperately the man wanted to believe, and He responded by healing his son.

Jesus also knows how desperately you want to believe and how you battle your doubts and fears. Belief is not the result of a convincing intellectual argument, but an act of your will. It is choosing every day to activate your faith through prayer, ignoring your feelings, surrendering everything to God, and expecting Him to answer. The power of God plus a mustard seed of faith *can* move your mountain. Come to Him in prayer with an attitude of complete dependence. Pray in faith to see your healing come. Ask Him to help you not to doubt.

# Prayer

*God, like the father in this story, I desperately want to believe! I have read about Your healing miracles when You walked this earth with Your disciples. I have heard amazing stories about Your healing power today. Cancer is healed, the crippled rise up from their wheelchairs and walk, the blind see, the deaf hear, and the captives are set free! Even if I haven't seen these miracles with my own eyes, I want to believe the testimonies of those who have seen. You rebuked Your disciples when they refused to believe those who had seen You after You had risen from the dead (Mark 16:14). Even after You appeared before them in Your resurrected body, they still doubted (Luke 24:41). But You said to Thomas, "Blessed are those who believe without seeing me" (John 20:29). Lord, help me to believe even though I have not seen.*

*You have examined my heart, and You know everything about me. I can hide nothing from You. You know when I sit down or stand up. You know my every thought. You know what I am going to say even before I say it (Psalm 139:1–4). You know my doubts and fears, and You know how desperately I want to believe. Honor the desire of my heart, Lord! I want more faith. I want to believe. I want to believe my miracle is possible. Help me not to doubt!*

# Reckless Hope

*Bartimaeus threw aside his coat, jumped up, and came to Jesus. "What do you want me to do for you?" Jesus asked. "My Rabbi," the blind man said, "I want to see!" And Jesus said to him, "Go, for your faith has healed you." Instantly the man could see, and he followed Jesus down the road.*

MARK 10:50–52

Bartimaeus sat beside the road into Jericho. His blindness had forced him to beg for as long as he could remember. He wasn't alone. Others like him suffered crippling diseases or disabilities that rendered them unable to make an honest living. The people had long ago forgotten their obligation to care for them. He didn't give much thought to why he was blind. Some told him it was a curse from God for his sin, but it really didn't matter. All he knew was that every day his life depended on his ability to talk some passerby into parting with a few coins. He liked the traffic on this particular road because he was able to make contact with travelers on their way to Jerusalem.

Suddenly, he heard the noise of a crowd going past. Sensing opportunity, he pressed them to find out what was happening. When they told him Jesus of Nazareth was passing by, he instantly began shouting, "Jesus, Son of David, have mercy on me!" The crowd ahead of Jesus tried to hush him, but he only shouted louder. He persisted until Jesus stopped and ordered that he be brought to Him. Throwing down his coat with reckless abandon, he jumped up and rushed over to Jesus. "What do you want Me to do for you?" asked Jesus. Bartimaeus shouted in reply, "Lord, I want to see!"

As soon as Jesus said the words "Go, for your faith has

healed you," the thick veil that had covered Bartimaeus's eyes for a lifetime instantly lifted, and light flooded into the darkness. He blinked several times to let his eyes adjust. He could see! The people, the road, the landscape, the sky—everything came alive with color! He looked directly into the eyes of the Teacher, and he could do only one thing—follow Him (Mark 10:46–52).

Bartimaeus had little hope of escaping his situation, but he had hope in the Messiah. By calling Him "Son of David," Bartimaeus acknowledged Jesus as the long-awaited Messiah the scriptures foretold would be a descendant of King David (Isaiah 9:7). He shamelessly called out for Jesus' attention in spite of the crowd's rebuke. Without thinking, he threw down his coat—most likely his only possession—to come to Jesus with his request. He was determined not to let Jesus pass him by without receiving His healing, and his reckless faith gave him sight. He had no choice but to follow Jesus.

Bartimaeus, a blind man, recognized Jesus as the long-awaited Messiah, while the religious leaders watched Him perform countless miracles and were blind to His identity. Don't let Him pass you by. Ask Him to open your eyes. Be bold and tell Him exactly what you want Him to do for you. He is the Son of David, your Savior and King! Cry out to Him for mercy. Cry out to Him and be healed. Pursue Him with a reckless hope.

# Prayer

*Lord, I'm just another blind Bartimaeus. Open my eyes so I can see who You really are! I want to know You as Mighty God, Everlasting Father, and Prince of Peace. Your ever-expanding government will never end, and You will rule forever with fairness and justice from the throne of Your ancestor David (Isaiah 9:6–7)! You are my Savior and Redeemer. I know these things in my head, Lord, but I want more. Open my eyes so I can see You with my heart.*

*Lord, I want a reckless hope like Bartimaeus's. Forgive me if I have been holding back out of ignorance, denial, or concern for what others might think of me. Give me the boldness to call out Your name and tell you exactly what I need. I surrender everything that separates me from You so I can experience Your presence, hear Your voice, and receive Your blessings. I want to follow You, Lord. I want to follow You all the days of my life. Help me persist with a reckless hope in my pursuit of You. Son of David, have mercy on me! Don't pass me by. I want to be healed!*

# He Is God

*Jesus took the blind man by the hand and led him out of the village. Then, spitting on the man's eyes, he laid his hands on him and asked, "Can you see anything now?" The man looked around. "Yes," he said, "I see people, but I can't see them very clearly. They look like trees walking around." Then Jesus placed his hands on the man's eyes again, and his eyes were opened. His sight was completely restored, and he could see everything clearly.*
MARK 8:23–25

"Come quickly! The Healer is here!" they shouted. He was resting in the village by the side of the road when he heard their voices. He felt several hands pull him to his feet. Surrounding him on all sides, they hurried him down the road. "Jesus has come to Bethsaida!" they said. "Let's ask Him to touch you and make you see!" He had heard about this man Jesus. Some said He was the Messiah who would come and save them from their Roman oppressors. There were stories of His preaching throughout the villages. Everywhere He went, the blind could see, the lame walked, the lepers were cured, and the deaf could hear—all by a touch of His hand. *If He touches me, I will be healed, too!* He hurried along with his friends, anticipating the miracle that could change his life forever.

They came to a stop, and he could hear the sounds of a larger crowd. Pushing through the crowd, he joined them in clamoring around the Healer he couldn't see. "Teacher, this man is blind. Please touch him and heal him. Please, Teacher, please restore his sight!" his friends begged. The pleading continued until he felt Jesus take his hand. He fully expected to be healed at that moment, but instead, Jesus led him silently away from the crowd. *Where are we going?*

The voices of the crowd faded as they approached the outskirts of the village. Jesus stopped and turned him. And then He did the strangest thing. *Ptuh!* He spit on his eyes! *What is He doing?* Jesus laid hands on him and asked, "Can you see anything now?" To his amazement, the darkness was gone! He blinked, straining to see, but the images were unclear. He thought he could see people, but their blurred bodies resembled tree trunks and their arms looked like branches. *Thank You, Jesus!* He felt Jesus touch his eyes again. This time, his vision cleared and the images were sharp. His sight was completely restored. He could see (Mark 8:22–26)!

This man's healing did not come in the way he expected. Jesus took him outside the village away from the people, and He spit on his eyes. He didn't heal him right away. He chose to heal the man in stages. In doing so, He may have wanted to show His followers that healing is not always instantaneous. His divine power over sickness sometimes works gradually, and not always on our timetable or in the way we expect. Or He may have wanted to show us that blessing flows from a place of intimacy when we make time to be alone with Him.

Don't be discouraged if the physical manifestation of your healing comes slowly or in stages. Instead, choose to be thankful in each step of the process. God has the entire spiritual and material realm at His disposal, and He has purposes far greater than your human mind can understand. Let Him pull you away from the crowd, away from everything else that competes for your attention. He is God, the Creator of all things. He is God, without beginning or end (Psalm 90:2). In all seasons, He is God.

# Prayer

*Oh Lord my God, how great You are! I bow low before Your feet for You are just and holy. Your thoughts are completely different from mine, and Your ways are far beyond anything I can imagine. For just as the heavens are higher than the earth, so are Your ways higher than my ways, and Your thoughts higher than my thoughts (Isaiah 55:8–9). Lord, forgive me for trying to figure out all Your ways. Forgive me for presuming to know how You will move in a certain situation. I know You will not be limited by my human understanding. There are some things I will never understand until I meet You face-to-face. Why would I ever want to worship a God whose thoughts and ways are no higher than mine? Oh God, how great You are!*

*Lord, I know You have the power to heal me instantly. However You bring healing to my body, I know You have a plan and a greater purpose that will bring You glory. Like the blind man in the story, take me "outside the village" where I can be alone with You and away from the things that crowd You out of my life. Take me to that place of intimacy with You where my healing can be complete, in Your perfect time and in Your perfect way. Thank You, Lord, for You are good! Your faithfulness endures forever. I praise You, my King! I bless Your name forever and ever (Psalm 145:1). You are righteous in everything You do, even when I don't understand. You are God.*

## Jehovah-Rapha: Jeff's Story

Jeff waited in the exam room for the doctor to come, passing the time by flipping aimlessly through the latest edition of *Prevention* magazine. Waiting was something he had grown used to over the past two years—waiting for doctors; waiting for chemo to drip from the medication bag through his port and into his body; waiting for scans and test results; waiting for healing to come.

He had already defied the medical odds. Most people with stage 4 colon cancer weren't doing nearly as well at this point in the game. Fifty chemo sessions and two years after his diagnosis, he was still fighting. It wasn't an ordinary fight. It was God's battle, not his. And most of the time, he thought God was winning. The doctor couldn't believe he was still working full-time, playing pickup basketball once a week, and living a nearly normal life. Well, as normal as life could be with chemo every other week and all its side effects. Even his blood counts remained normal. Usually the chemo destroys healthy cells along with the cancer cells, often driving blood counts to dangerously low levels. His counts were consistently at normal, pre-chemo levels. *Praise Him!*

The tumors in his colon and liver were inoperable. Until the cancer disappeared or shrunk to a level where surgery became an option, biweekly chemo would be a routine part of his life. Complete healing of stage 4 cancer was a tall order for the medical realm. But not for God. *With Him, anything is possible.* He smiled at the thought.

His faith sustained him and his family throughout

this battle. He truly loved the Lord with all his heart, soul, and mind. He loved God's Word and found strength in reading and meditating on it every day. He felt so blessed to be part of a faith-filled family. God had given him a beautiful wife and three sons. He loved the times they prayed and studied the Bible together. Strangely, this disease had brought them closer to one another and to God. He met regularly with other believers to receive healing prayer and pray for those suffering from cancer and other life difficulties. He knew his story and his strength inspired them. He always made it clear that the strength they witnessed was not his own. Tears came to his eyes at the thought of God's faithfulness.

Cancer had humbled him. He had grown fully dependent on God and acquired a deep desire to live in His presence. He had discovered the secret of abiding. In this intimate place with God, he found love, peace, and supernatural joy in the midst of his suffering. In this secret place, he found the hope that sustained him. He came to desire the sweet presence of Jesus even more than his healing. He wanted his healing to glorify God and to become a witness of His power and goodness for all to see. Every day, God seemed to reveal more of Himself. Just like the leper who knew God could heal him if He wanted to, he had heard God say, "I want to." He walked every day in divine health, experiencing a healing that had not yet manifested in his physical body.

Lost in his thoughts, he barely noticed the soft rap on the door and the doctor coming into the examination room. The doctor greeted him with the usual hug. After this long, a guy could become good friends with his physician. The doctor wasted no time. "We have good news, Jeff! The large tumor in your colon appears to be dead. Several other tumors in your liver are dead or in the process of dying. But we have some small spots in your lung we have to tackle next."

Jeff smiled. *Faithful again. Thank You, Jesus.* While the doctor explained the next plan of attack, Jeff knew deep in his spirit that God would complete the work He had started. Either way, he wins.

# Hope Restored

*When the Lord saw her, his heart overflowed with compassion.*
*"Don't cry!" he said. Then he walked over to the coffin and touched it,*
*and the bearers stopped. "Young man," he said, "I tell you, get up."*
*Then the dead boy sat up and began to talk!*
LUKE 7:13–15

Surrounded and held by mourning relatives and villagers, she rested her red and swollen eyes on the coffin a few steps in front of her. First her husband, and now her only son; the child she had carried in her womb, nursed at her breast, cared for, loved, and nurtured. She'd had so much hope for him and the man he would become. And now, all her hopes were dead. Fresh tears spilled from her puffy eyes and rolled down her cheeks.

She dared not think of her future without him. Not only was he the son she cherished, but he represented her last means of support. She was past childbearing age and would probably never marry again. She pushed the thought of being penniless, alone, and begging for food out of her mind. For now, she kept her eyes planted on the coffin as the growing procession of mourners made its way through the town to the village gates.

At the gates, she saw a large crowd approaching the village. The people were captivated by a man in front of the crowd, and they clamored to get closer to Him, competing for His attention. But He was focused on the coffin. Then His eyes searched the crowd and found hers. He saw the depth of her grief and despair, and immediately, His heart overflowed with compassion. "Don't cry!" He said. Overwhelmed by a strange sense of peace, she watched Him walk over to the coffin and touch it. The bearers stopped and the man spoke directly to her dead son. "Young man," He said, "I tell you, get up." She barely had time to process what was happening, when her dead son did just that. He got up and began to talk. Shock, disbelief, and joy collided all at once as her knees buckled and she dropped to the ground. Did she dare believe what was happening before her very eyes? Did this strange man actually raise her son from the dead (Luke 7:11–16)?

Yes. He had done it before and He would do it again. Scripture recounts three miraculous resurrections in the Old Testament (1 Kings 17:17–24; 2 Kings 4:35; 13:21). At least two more people were raised from the dead by Jesus (Matthew 9:25; John 11:43–44), and many saints were resurrected at His crucifixion (Matthew 27:52–53). Both Peter and Paul raised a person from the dead (Acts 9:36–42; 20:9–12). Even today, there are stories of the dead being raised through the ministry of missionaries such as Heidi and Rolland Baker in Mozambique, and cardiologist Dr. Chauncey Crandall has witnessed the resurrection power of Jesus Christ at work in his own hospital (*Raising the Dead: A Doctor Encounters the Miraculous*, FaithWords, 2012).

Raising the dead is a stunning miracle, but the resurrection of Jesus is the greatest miracle of all. Just as He had compassion for this woman when her hope was dead, our Father in heaven has compassion for you. When the whole world was dead to sin and your future was hopeless, He sent His Son to raise you to life with Him (Ephesians 2:1, 4–7). He restored your hope for all eternity.

# Prayer

*Lord, sometimes I feel hopeless like this woman who lost her only son. Tears blind my eyes and I can't see anything good in my future. Lord, You know me better than I know myself. You know what lies ahead, because You laid out every moment of my life before a single day had passed (Psalm 139:16). Thank You for understanding all my fears and my deepest longings. Thank You for having compassion on me and restoring my hope when I see nothing but darkness in front of me. Thank You for raising my hope from the dead.*

*Jesus, I trust You to make me well again. You have the power to heal, the power to restore, and the power to raise the dead. Thank You, Jesus, that through Your resurrection, I am assured of the ultimate healing, a healing bought and paid for by Your blood. I know that my present body is perishable and that death will remain the final earthly human condition until the complete coming of Your Kingdom and the resurrection of all believers (1 Corinthians 15:42–44, 51–55). On that day, I will get up! I will praise You forever with all my heart, all my soul, and all my strength. Praise You, Jesus! You are my only hope.*

# Believe and Receive

*Looking straight at him, Paul realized he had faith to be healed.*
*So Paul called to him in a loud voice, "Stand up!" And the*
*man jumped to his feet and started walking.*
Acts 14:9–10

The man with the crippled feet listened attentively to these two followers of Jesus. As he listened to them preach, he marveled at their boldness. They preached with such authority, such certainty that Jesus was truly the Messiah and that God was offering salvation to anyone, Jew or Gentile, who came to Him through Jesus. He heard these men had done many miraculous signs and wonders in the neighboring town of Iconium in Galatia, but their preaching caused controversy. They were forced to run for their lives to his hometown of Lystra when a murderous mob decided to attack and stone them to death. Nothing seemed to stop them from preaching this good news.

He had been crippled since birth. He had never walked. As he listened to their words, something deep inside him began to stir. What if it was true? What if this Jesus truly was the Son of God who came to take away the sins of the world? What if He had the compassion and power to heal and restore? They said that by the power of His name, the blind see, the lepers are cured, the deaf hear, and the lame walk. *The lame walk. What if. . . What if I could walk?* His heart filled with hope at the thought of a completely changed life—no more crutches, no longer using his knees as feet, no more dragging his worthless limbs through the dirt. He saw himself walking.

At that moment, Paul noticed him. Paul looked into his eyes and could see he had the faith to be healed. He stopped his preaching and called out in a loud voice to the crippled man, "Stand up!" Without thinking, he found himself jumping to his feet. He could walk! Praise Jesus, he could walk (Acts 14:8–10)!

The Holy Spirit gave Paul the knowledge that this crippled man had taken God at His word. He believed that Jesus could make him walk. He believed before he received. Jesus said we can pray for anything, and if we believe that we've received it, it will be ours (Mark 11:24). But most of us pray backwards. We lift up our requests to God and wait for the answers to manifest. When we receive an answer, *then* we believe. Paul didn't even have to pray for this man. He simply asked for the evidence of what this man believed to be revealed. He proclaimed out loud what had already been done in heaven.

Like this crippled man, you can rise up in faith and take what you believe rightfully belongs to you. You can take by faith what God has promised and hold on to it for dear life. You can believe and receive.

# Prayer

*Father God, I know healing is no problem for You. Help me have faith like this crippled man. Help me to take You at Your word, to rise up in faith and take hold of Your promises. Help me to see myself healed and to see myself in perfect health. Help me not to focus on my current circumstances, but to believe the eternal things that are not seen (2 Corinthians 4:18). Please give me faith to "[call] those things which do not exist as though they did" (Romans 4:17 NKJV). When I read Your Word, help me to truly believe You are speaking to me and that I can have all that You promise. Help me to believe and then receive.*

*When we pray as You taught us, that "Your will be done on earth as it is in heaven," we are praying for the heavenly reality to be evidenced here on earth. Lord, there is no sickness in heaven. If this condition that I suffer from cannot exist in heaven, then it cannot exist here. Right now, I call heaven to earth. I see myself healed and restored. I take You at Your word. And I ask for evidence of what I believe to be revealed. I stand up in faith and take what rightfully belongs to me. Lord, I believe. I receive by faith all that You freely give.*

# His Redemptive Grace

*Then Jesus turned to the paralyzed man and said, "Stand up,
pick up your mat, and go home!" And the man jumped up,
grabbed his mat, and walked out through the stunned onlookers.*
MARK 2:10–12

They said Jesus was back. News like this traveled fast, even in a densely populated city like Capernaum. It really didn't matter to him. He had grown accustomed to his handicap. The paralysis immobilized him, but the town was wealthy enough and he managed to get by. A man like him couldn't expect much more. But his friends had other ideas. Jesus was teaching in the home of His host, and they had insisted on taking him to the gathering. They knew Jesus had the power to heal and they didn't want him to miss out. All four of them had come to fetch him. They scooped up the mat where he'd spent most of his life and rushed through the city's narrow streets to the house where Jesus was teaching.

To their dismay, the house was packed when they arrived, and even the outside door was blocked with people. There was no way they could push through the crowd to reach Jesus. Sighing, he assumed they would just take him back home to the life he knew and began to thank them for hoping for more, but his four friends were on a mission. "The roof!" one of them cried. They quickly located the narrow outside stairway that led to the rooftop and made their way up the stairs. By this time, he was confused. *What in the world are they thinking?*

In answer to his thoughts, one of his friends exclaimed, "We can lower you through the roof and get you close to the

Teacher!" He watched in amazement as they dug frantically at the hardened mud and straw tiles until the hole was big enough to fit him through. With him still on his mat, they grabbed the attached ropes and lowered him into the room. People scrambled aside and the next thing he knew, he was staring into the very face of Jesus.

He knew at that moment something life changing was about to happen. His eyes searched the Teacher's face, trying to make sense of the way he felt inside. Whatever it was, his heart filled with gratitude for the four friends who made sure he wouldn't miss it. Jesus simply smiled and said, "Son, your sins are forgiven." He felt as though invisible chains were dropping off his body, chains that had held him captive all his life. He felt lighter. He felt free. He felt love. And he had a strange sense that more was coming. Judging from the gasps and indignant murmurs of the Pharisees and teachers of religious law who stood watching, they didn't share his joy.

Jesus seemed to know what they were thinking. Unfazed, he said, "Is it easier to say 'Your sins are forgiven,' or 'Stand up and walk'? So I will prove to you that the Son of Man has the authority on earth to forgive sins." Then Jesus turned to the paralyzed man and said, "Stand up, pick up your mat, and go home!" In an instant, feeling returned to his limbs and he jumped to his feet. *I'm saved, I'm healed!* (Mark 2:1–12).

It was the faith of these four friends, not the faith of the paralyzed man, that impressed Jesus. They saw their friend's need and took drastic action. You can take heart that even when your own faith falters, the faith of others can move the heart of God on your behalf. Jesus responded to their faith by healing their paralyzed friend, but first, He forgave his sins. The Pharisees accused Jesus of blasphemy because only God had the power to forgive sins, and they had no idea who

He was. Jesus demonstrated God's power to heal and that forgiveness of sin *and* physical healing are both a part of His redemptive grace. His grace can change your life forever.

## Prayer

*Lord, forgive me when I get tired of waiting for my breakthrough to come and I expect much less than You have planned for me. Thank You for the friends who stand in the gap for me when my faith is weak. Thank You that they won't give up hope, even when I have settled for hopelessness, and that they will do whatever is necessary to help me keep my eyes on Your face and Your power to heal and restore.*

*Lord, I thank You for Your redemptive grace. You forgive all my sins, You heal all my diseases, and You redeem my life from destruction. You sacrificed so much to heal my spirit, soul, and body. Help me to know and understand all of this in my heart. I want to gaze into Your face. I want to know You. More of Your presence, more of Your promises, more of Your power. More of You.*

# Walking in the Fullness

*"I came that they may have and enjoy life,*
*and have it in abundance [to the full, till it overflows]."*
JOHN 10:10 AMP

Somewhat agitated, Phyllis marched up to the speaker who had shared her testimony of how God healed her of cancer. "If it's true that God heals today," she said, "then my husband would still be here. I really think the abundant life Jesus spoke of in John 10:10 is all about the life that is waiting for us in heaven."

When Jesus walked the earth, people didn't seem to have a problem accepting and believing that He could heal the sick. Led by the teachings of the Pharisees and teachers of religious law, they didn't believe He had the power to forgive their sins and save their souls. Ironically, Christians today have no issues with Jesus as the way to heaven through the forgiveness of their sin. But like Phyllis, they often struggle to believe He still heals the sick. Then as well as today, Jesus wants you to experience the completeness of your salvation. He wants you to live the abundant life of freedom He won for you on the cross. He wants you to walk in the fullness of life, till it overflows.

Phyllis believed that all this abundance is waiting for us in heaven. On this side of eternity, we're supposed to grit our teeth and bear all that life throws at us, longing for the relief that will come only on that day when we go home to Jesus. To a certain extent, this is true. Death will remain the final earthly human condition until the complete coming of the Kingdom and the resurrection (1 Corinthians 15:51–55). The

Holy Spirit within us is a foretaste of this future glory, and we all eagerly wait for the day when God will give us our *full* rights as His children (Romans 8:23). However, if waiting passively for heaven is our entire Christian experience, we can miss out on the abundant life Jesus won for us here on earth, as well as our call and purpose to advance the Kingdom of God.

Walking in this fullness today begins with believing that your healing, like the gift of eternal life, is part of the atonement given by grace through faith in Christ. Isaiah prophesied that Jesus took your sicknesses and removed your diseases. He was beaten so you could be whole, and you were healed by His stripes (Isaiah 53:4–5). Matthew said that when Jesus cast out evil spirits and healed all the sick, He fulfilled these words spoken through the prophet Isaiah (Matthew 8:16–17). In the early church, the apostles continued to show that healing was a critical part of God's message to the world (Acts 4:29–30; Romans 15:18–19). In other words, God considers your healing a "done deal."

The fullness of your salvation is captured in one Greek word: *sozo*. This word is used 110 times in the New Testament and means "to save or make well or whole." By using it in different contexts to refer to three aspects of salvation, the New Testament writers showed the completeness of the word. For example, *sozo* means saved from eternal destruction in Romans 10:9 (NIV): "If you declare with your mouth, 'Jesus is Lord,' and believe in your heart that God raised him from the dead, you will be saved [*sozo*]." *Sozo* refers to physical healing in Matthew 9:22: "Jesus turned around, and when he saw her he said, 'Daughter, be encouraged! Your faith has made you well [*sozo*].' And the woman was healed [*sozo*] at that moment." And in Luke 8:36 (NIV), *sozo* refers to inner healing and freedom from strongholds: "Those who had seen it told the people how the demon-possessed man had been cured [*sozo*]."

Jesus died so you could live with Him forever in paradise, an abundant life beyond anything you could ask or imagine (1 Corinthians 2:9). But His sacred gift of eternal life began the moment you first believed. In Him, you can have life to the full, till it overflows: salvation from eternal destruction, physical healing, and freedom from demonic strongholds. He wants you to walk in the fullness.

## Prayer

*Lord, I can't begin to imagine the price You paid so I can be saved, healed, and made whole. Forgive me if I have had a limited understanding of Your gift of salvation, or have doubted that physical healing, like the gift of eternal life, has already been done for me. I know the assurance of spending eternity with You in heaven is the greatest gift of all, but I want more. I want to receive everything You died for, all You won for me on the cross. I want the full return for Your suffering to be manifest in my life on both sides of heaven.*

*Holy Spirit, please show me if I have believed any lies about You or lies about myself that have hindered my ability to wait in Your presence, believe in Your goodness, and receive Your love and blessing. Lord, open my eyes and reveal Your truth. I want to know You, Lord. I want to personally know You as Lord of my Salvation, my Deliverer, and my Healer.* Sozo *me, Lord. Show me how to walk in the fullness till it overflows.*

# The Promise of God

*He rolled up the scroll, handed it back to the attendant, and sat down. All eyes in the synagogue looked at him intently. Then he began to speak to them. "The Scripture you've just heard has been fulfilled this very day!"*
Luke 4:20–21

Josias took his place in the synagogue and waited for the service to begin. He looked forward to worshipping and hearing the Word of God on the Sabbath. He still held out hope that someday, things would be different. The heavy yoke on their backs would be lifted and they would finally be free from their Roman oppressors. He prayed that "someday" would be in his lifetime. He longed for the day God would bring justice to Israel and they would no longer live as a poor and conquered people.

During opening prayers, his eyes searched the room for the visitor who would be teaching today. Jesus, son of Joseph and Mary, had been brought up right here in the village of Nazareth. Many in the village knew Him, and He had worked as a carpenter for many. People said He had been traveling around Galilee teaching in all the villages and was praised by everyone. Some said He had even performed miracles in Capernaum. Now He had returned to the city where He had been brought up to teach in His own synagogue.

When it was time to read from the Prophets, the attendant handed the scroll of Isaiah to Jesus. He stood, unrolled the scroll, and began to read: "The Spirit of the LORD is upon me, for he has anointed me to bring Good News to the poor. He has sent me to proclaim that captives will be released, that the blind will see, that the oppressed will be set free, and that the time of the LORD's favor has come."

When He finished, He rolled up the scroll, handed it back to the attendant, and sat down, preparing to teach. All eyes in the synagogue looked at Him intently. Josias wondered how He would explain what He had just read. To the crowd's amazement, Jesus simply said: "The Scripture you've just heard has been fulfilled this very day!"

His heart jumped. *Can this be?* As Jesus continued to speak, he felt the goodness and grace of God in His announcement. His hope began to rise. *Can this man really be our Messiah?* "How can this be? Is this not Joseph's son, the carpenter?" the crowd murmured. Josias watched their mood shift from amazement to anger when Jesus made it clear He was not about to prove His claim by doing miracles like He had done in Capernaum. Worse yet, He expressed God's heart for the unclean Gentiles! The furious crowd charged at Jesus. Josias watched. . .and wondered (Luke 4:16–28).

Is Jesus the promise of God? When Jesus quoted Isaiah 61:1–2, He announced His mission to the world—He was the One who would bring Isaiah's prophecy to pass, and the time was now. Their long-awaited Messiah had come to break the power of sin and death and begin God's personal reign on the earth. Jesus was anointed by God to minister and preach and proclaim the good news of the Kingdom. The Kingdom of God would bring freedom, healing, and restoration and would reverse the effects of Satan's presence in the world. It was the beginning of the fulfillment of God's promise, and Jesus was the Source of the fulfillment. Eventually, His ministry would bring total restoration and release to all creation (Romans 8:18–39; Revelation 21–22). But His announcement in the synagogue made all these promises possible now.

Josias, a fictitious worshipper, could have been anyone in the synagogue that day. Jesus' outrageous claims brought a moment of decision to all who heard, and the crowd's reaction is a snapshot of His entire ministry. God's message, then and now, is often met with rejection. They couldn't imagine that a carpenter's son from their hometown could be the one God chose to save them. Josias was left wondering. He was left to make a choice, and so are we. No fence-straddling is possible. Either Jesus *is* the promise of God, the Messiah who brings healing and restoration and destroys the works of the enemy, or He's not.

## Prayer

*Lord, sometimes I feel that same yoke of oppression as the Israelites in Jesus' day. I long for a time when things will be different, when You will deliver me from all my problems and heal my body, soul, and spirit. Forgive me when I forget that You, Jesus, are God's Chosen One, the promised Messiah, the fulfillment of all God's promises. I'm sorry when I focus on the works of the enemy instead of You, the Anointed One who came to break the power of sin and death.*

*Lord, I believe Your Kingdom has come on earth. In Your Kingdom, the captives are released, the blind will see, and the oppressed are set free. The coming of Your Kingdom changed everything and makes all these things possible in my life today: freedom, healing, and restoration. You are indeed the Promise of God, the Messiah.*

## Jehovah-Rapha: Sandy's Story

Sandy fidgeted in her seat, trying to get comfortable. These padded theater-style seats were a lot better than the wooden pews in their old church. It was a good thing, because her rheumatoid arthritis had grown significantly more crippling over the years. What started in her hands and feet had moved to her knees, hips, and shoulders. The medication took the edge off the swollen, warm, tender joints, but the pain was always there in the background. She couldn't remember the last time she woke in the morning without being nearly immobilized by the stiffness. She looked down at her hands, studying the bulging red knuckles and crooked fingers, annoyed at the difficulty she was having just grasping a pen to take notes on the sermon.

The pastor was ready to give the final blessing when he reminded the congregation that prayer ministers were waiting in the front to pray for anything they might need or request. She had received prayer before. She loved the Lord and believed He could heal her, or at least take away the pain. Even though the symptoms persisted, she hadn't given up hope, even after eighteen years of progressive disease. Today, she would go up front again and bring her husband with her. He was a kind and caring man, and he longed for her to get some relief from the pain.

They approached a couple they hadn't prayed with before. As usual, she felt welcomed by their warm greeting. They asked how they could pray and she repeated her story. Eighteen years ago, she awakened to tender, swollen joints and pain throughout her body. She could barely get out of bed. It had come on suddenly out of nowhere. Her doctor diagnosed rheumatoid arthritis, and she had been battling the worsening condition ever since with the latest drugs and therapies.

Sandy closed her eyes, ready to receive prayer, when one of the prayer ministers asked an interesting question. "Was anything traumatic going on in your life during the time these symptoms first appeared?" She thought about her life back then, her failed marriage, and how the Lord had blessed her with this good man who stood at her side and carried her through the trauma of a messy divorce. The prayer minister spoke into the silence of her thoughts. "If you are comfortable, I'd like you to ask God if there is anything He wants to bring into your mind about this time in your life," she said.

Sandy repeated the minister's prayer. Almost at once, the memories flooded back into her mind: the stinging words, the shouting, the hurt and rejection. Her husband was leaving her. She had no clue he was having an affair. He was moving out and seeking a divorce. He had found someone else, and he was not interested in getting counseling or saving the marriage. Her world crashed. She cried for days and couldn't sleep. After pure exhaustion finally forced her to sleep, she woke up that morning with all the physical symptoms of arthritis.

Then the prayer minister gently asked her the question she dreaded most: "Have you forgiven your ex-husband?" Sandy looked down and murmured, "I've tried. It's hard." Understanding, the prayer minister agreed. "Yes, I know. Jesus knows, too. He is no stranger to your pain. He commands forgiveness because He knows how unforgiveness can hold us in bondage, block our blessing, and cause both physical illness and mental stress. He came to set us free from the prison of bitterness. He has the power to forgive when we can't." She smiled and her voice lowered. "Forgiveness is a choice, you know. It's not a feeling. It doesn't mean what he did to you was okay. He still owes you the debt to be a faithful husband. Forgiveness means you are choosing to forgive the debt he owes you and releasing him to God. You are no longer judging him, but letting God be the judge. You are choosing to let God heal your pain, and not expecting your relief to come any other way."

Tears streamed down Sandy's cheeks. "Can you choose to forgive him? To release him to God?" the prayer minister asked. "Yes, I'm ready," Sandy said. With the prayer minister guiding her words, she prayed, "Father, I choose to forgive the debt my ex-husband owes me. I release him to You, Lord. Please forgive me for harboring bitterness against him all these years." At that moment, she felt a weight lifting off her shoulders. She felt lighter. Immediately, the two prayer ministers began to pray for physical healing. They each held one of her hands while they prayed, and she began to feel heat flow through her hands and travel up her arms. As they slowly released her hands, she was stunned to see her fingers were straighter. The tight, shiny red skin had turned flesh color, and the knuckles appeared to be nearly normal size. She wiggled her fingers. *No pain! Thank You, Jesus!*

She knew there was more to come. During additional ministry time with a team of trained inner healing ministers, the Lord's power touched the deepest places of her wounding. He replaced lies she believed about herself with the truth about her identity and worthiness as a beloved daughter of the King. He replaced misconceptions she had about Father God with the truth of His goodness and passionate love for her. She released her fear of abandonment to the only One who would never leave or forsake her. Eventually her entire body was completely free from the symptoms of arthritis. Sandy was completely healed and restored by the grace and power of Jehovah-Rapha, the God who heals.

# He Healed Them All

*A vast crowd brought to him people who were lame,*
*blind, crippled, those who couldn't speak, and many others.*
*They laid them before Jesus, and he healed them all.*
MATTHEW 15:30

Jenny's eyes rested on the scripture she had just read. Over and over she repeated the same words until they began to flash across her mind like a scrolling banner ad in lights. *He healed them all. He healed them all. He healed them all.* She had been doctoring for months. The tumor in her brain was large and inoperable. Medically, the only hope was to shrink it and remove as much as possible, although the surgery would be risky. Every visit to the doctor was the same discouraging news: *The tumor is still there. It's shrinking, but it's still there.* She wanted it gone. She wanted this intruder out of her body. She had prayed. Oh, how she had prayed. Others prayed for her. Multiple times they had laid hands on her and anointed her with oil. She had felt the Spirit of God move through their prayer. *The tumor is still there. But Jesus healed them all. Jesus, why not me?*

Whether in individual encounters or when ministering to the masses, Jesus didn't refuse to heal anyone who came to Him or was brought to Him by loved ones. He healed them *all* (Matthew 4:24; 8:16; 12:15; 14:36; Mark 6:56; Luke 4:40). It was such a priority that 25 percent of the Gospels focus on His healing ministry, and we know from scripture that He is the same yesterday, today, and forever (Hebrews 13:8). If Jesus healed them all, and if He never changes, Jenny asks for all of us, *Jesus, why not me? Why not my loved one?*

Quite simply, there can be hindrances to healing that our human minds cannot explain. Even the best pastors and theologians cannot provide all the answers to these questions. For centuries since the early church, when healing prayer has not resulted in physical healing, our tendency has been to find human explanations to make sense of our circumstances. In essence, we make up things about God and His nature that are not founded in scripture. For example, explanations like "It's not God's will to heal," or "God doesn't heal today," or "I am unworthy of being healed" are in direct conflict with the goodness of God and the nature of Jesus Christ. We must never base theology on our experience. Jesus must be our standard for all truth. In his Facebook post on May 5, 2014, Bill Johnson, senior leader at Bethel Church in Redding, California, put it this way: "I will not sacrifice my knowledge of the goodness of God on the altar of human reasoning so I can have an explanation for a seemingly unanswered prayer."

While on this earth, we will live in a constant tension between the truth of God's Word and the facts surrounding our circumstances. While it may seem like our prayers go unanswered, the good news is that healing prayer is always effective for believers. God will always complete the good work He has begun—in Jenny and in you (Philippians 1:6). God heals here and now in this world, so we can pray with great expectancy. God heals in eternity what is not healed here and now, so we can pray with deep confidence (1 Corinthians 15:42–44, 51–55; 2 Corinthians 4:16).

So keep praying. Keep believing for more. Keep your eyes focused on Jesus so that what you see and experience around you does not shake your faith in what you know to be true. Continue to trust God and His goodness, to know Him intimately as you seek a greater understanding of His redemptive grace. You are His child, and you are loved beyond measure. You have Jesus, the standard for all truth. And the truth is, He healed them all.

## Prayer

*Help me, Lord. I need Your strength to believe Your truth, especially when it doesn't align with my experience. Forgive me when I have allowed my circumstances to cause me to doubt or distort Your truth and Your goodness. Help me to stand firm so my faith isn't shaken when my circumstances appear to contradict Your Word. Help me to focus on Your truth and what You are doing, and not try to make sense of what I perceive You aren't doing. I know that even when I can't see the physical manifestation of my prayers, You are still good. You are still advocating for me in the heavenly realm.*

*Lord, help me to resist the enemy, to counter any influence he still holds against me and recover any blessing he has stolen from me. Jesus, I want to receive Your full reward (1 Peter 5:9; John 10:10). Thank You, Jesus, that You healed them all. Thank You that by Your stripes, You healed me. I trust You, Lord. I trust Your goodness. Your Word is truth.*

# Glory to God

*Jesus asked, "Didn't I heal ten men? Where are the other nine?*
*Has no one returned to give glory to God except this foreigner?"*
*And Jesus said to the man, "Stand up and go. Your faith has healed you."*
LUKE 17:17–19

One of ten men banished to the outskirts of the village on the border between Galilee and Samaria, he was the only Samaritan in the group—a foreigner from a race despised by the Jews as half-breed idolaters. But his ethnicity didn't matter anymore. Leprosy leveled the playing field. Jew or Samaritan, they all shared the same destiny. Barring a miracle, they would all live the same destitute, lonely life, separated from their families and the lives they once enjoyed. The law required that they stay away from others to prevent the contagious disease from spreading. If they needed something or had to come close, the law required that they announce themselves by shouting "Unclean!" repeatedly so the people could scatter and let them pass. It was humiliating. He longed to hold his family and children close again. He longed for touch, for community. As it stood, the only human contact he had was with these nine leprous Jews. It was no way to live, and it was no way to die.

Yes, he needed a miracle. And that's exactly what they were hoping for today. They heard Jesus was on His way to Jerusalem, so He would have to pass by their village. Jesus had healed multitudes of people, including those with leprosy, with a touch of His hand or simply by speaking the words. They had been watching for Him from a distance. As He entered the village, one of them shouted, "Ah, there He is!"

They all began crying out together, "Jesus, Master, have mercy on us!" Looking up and seeing the ten men, He simply said, "Go show yourselves to the priests."

Now, it was the law that if a leper thought his disease was gone, he had to go present himself to a priest to be examined, and the priest would declare him clean. Without pause, he, along with the other nine lepers, began running for the priests. And as they went, they were cleansed of their leprosy. When the Samaritan realized what had happened, he stopped in his tracks. He looked down at his clear skin. *Jesus, Jesus, I am healed! I am clean!* Overwhelmed with emotion, he turned and ran back to the place where Jesus had spoken to him and fell to the ground at His feet. "Praise God!" he shouted. "Thank You for healing me!" Jesus asked, "Didn't I heal ten men? Where are the other nine? Has no one returned to give glory to God except this foreigner?" And Jesus said to the man, "Stand up and go. Your faith has healed you" (Luke 17:11–19).

After the priest confirmed their healing, the other nine men probably ran through the city rejoicing and reuniting with their families and friends. Even though this man yearned for his family, too, he celebrated first by thanking Jesus and giving God all the glory for healing and restoration. He was clearly humbled by the mercy Jesus had shown him. Jesus responded to his gratitude and worshipful attitude by telling him the important role faith played in his healing.

Jesus sent these ten men to the priests before they were healed, and they simply believed Jesus. They didn't wait for the healing to manifest. By faith, they believed the priests would declare them clean. But by returning to Jesus, the Samaritan received more. Jesus used his gratitude to teach him more about Himself. Our worship, gratefulness, and humility will always release more spiritual revelation and a greater understanding of God's grace. When God shows His mercy and healing comes, thank Him first. Give glory to God.

## Prayer

*Father, like these ten lepers, I cry out for Your mercy. I am desperate to be healed and restored. Please give me a faith so strong that I can step out and take action and believe that my healing has come before I see the physical evidence! Help me to believe You at Your word.*

*Lord, forgive my ungratefulness and the times I have forgotten to give You the glory for every blessing and each answered prayer in my healing journey. I want to grow in my understanding of Your grace. I want to grow in my knowledge of You. I humble myself before You, Lord! I worship You! Thank You for Your mercy. Thank You for healing me! I give You the glory.*

# Hold Out Your Hand

*He looked around at them angrily and was deeply saddened by
their hard hearts. Then he said to the man, "Hold out your hand."
So the man held out his hand, and it was restored!*
MARK 3:5

It was another Sabbath day and Jesus was teaching. The
man looked down at his withered right hand, trying for the
hundredth time to move it, to feel something. But there was
nothing. No feeling and no movement. The lifeless hand
had rendered him helpless. His right forearm was a clumsy
substitute for a hand. It was difficult to grasp, hold, and
manipulate the basic objects necessary for daily living, let
alone to practice his trade. He thought about his former life
as a bricklayer and the satisfaction he had felt in his work.
Now he was forced to beg just to meet his basic needs.

His former life was gone for good, unless everything they
said about Jesus was true. Unless He really was the Messiah,
the Redeemer of Israel, and He really could heal the sick,
restore sight to the blind, cleanse the lepers, make the deaf
hear, cause the lame to walk, and raise the dead. He looked
up from his thoughts and realized Jesus was staring directly
at him. For a moment his heart started to race. *Jesus can heal
me.* And then he remembered. It was the Sabbath. The laws
forbade working on the Sabbath, unless lives were in danger.
And healing was like medicine, and practicing medicine was
working. He sighed. His life was not in danger. It was just
rendered useless by this worthless hand.

None of this escaped the notice of the Pharisees and
teachers of religious law. They saw what was going on and

were watching Jesus very closely, preparing to pounce on His next move. Jesus seemed to know exactly what they were thinking.

Finally, one of them asked Him, "Does the law permit a person to work by healing on the Sabbath?" Jesus answered, "If you had a sheep that fell into a well on the Sabbath, wouldn't you work to pull it out? Of course you would. And how much more valuable is a person than a sheep! Yes, the law permits a person to do good on the Sabbath."

The crippled man barely had time to process Jesus' answer when he heard Him say, "Come and stand in front of everyone." Without hesitation or any concern for the law or the religious leaders, he came to the front and stood. He saw both anger and grief in Jesus' face as He looked around the room at the teachers and Pharisees. Then Jesus said to him, "Hold out your hand." Again, he immediately obeyed. Holding out his hand, he looked down in amazement. It was normal! He wiggled his fingers and clenched his fist. *Praise Jesus, my hand is healed!* (Matthew 12:9–14; Mark 3:1–6).

By healing on the Sabbath, Jesus rebuked the Pharisees, who then became wild with rage and began plotting to kill Him. Their plan all along was to get Him to break their laws so they could arrest Him on charges that His power was not from God. Jesus was outraged at them for putting their laws above human needs. He could have waited for another day to heal the man's hand, but in doing so, He would have been submitting to their authority and agreeing that their rules were equal to God's law. He made it clear that God put people over petty rules.

The man who was healed took immediate action. He obeyed when Jesus told him to come and stand. Instead of holding back out of concern for breaking the law and unleashing the Pharisees' wrath, he stood with the only One who could heal him. He didn't believe God wanted him to live this way. God's nature didn't line up with the Pharisees' rules. So he stretched out his hand in faith, beyond man's rules and limitations, and received His healing.

You, too, are worth more to God than petty rules. He might be waiting for you to obey Him before you receive, to step out of your comfort zone, to do something counter-intuitive, to stretch beyond what seems possible, without worrying about the opinions of others. He might be waiting for you to hold out your hand.

## Prayer

*Lord, please show me if there are any areas in my healing journey where I have submitted to worldly rules, paradigms, norms, and limitations instead of Your mighty power. Forgive me if I have failed to take action out of fear, the opinions of others, or my own discomfort. Lord, please give me the boldness to step out in obedience when I know in my spirit what You want me to do. Help me to trust Your wisdom and understanding, and not my own (Proverbs 3:5–8).*

*Lord, I need Your courage to stretch beyond limitation, beyond what seems possible, beyond what feels comfortable. Holy Spirit, take me to higher places in my understanding of You and Your power. Help me to obey You, even when obedience feels counterintuitive. Help me to stand with You, the only One who can heal me. Lord, I hold out my hand.*

# He Wants You Well

*This is the confidence we have in approaching God: that if we ask anything according to his will, he hears us. And if we know that he hears us— whatever we ask—we know that we have what we asked of him.*

1 JOHN 5:14–15 NIV

"How can I pray for you today?" the prayer minister asked. Tanya lifted her head and her eyes filled with tears. Taking a deep breath, she began to explain how she had injured her back several years ago, how the injury was the root cause of her progressively worsening back problems. Over the years, she had tried chiropractors, physical therapists, and orthopedic specialists. The pain persisted and was often debilitating. The last doctor recommended a risky surgery. "I want God's will to be done. I want to be healed if it's His will," she said. The prayer minister gently asked, "If it's possible that God would not want to heal you, wouldn't you be acting outside His will by seeking healing through medicine?" "Well, no," she stammered. The prayer minister smiled. "Then you can approach God in prayer the very same way, knowing He wants you well."

"Lord, if it be Your will. . ." We often add this caveat to our prayers out of dependence and reverence for God and His sovereign will. Sometimes, it's very appropriate to do so, especially when our heart's desire is to be in alignment with God's plan. But sometimes, we pray an "if it be Your will" prayer to give ourselves an out, rather than as an act of full surrender. With this type of prayer, there is no need to stand in faith that we will receive what we ask for. It's almost like preparing ourselves in advance for Him to say no. Then, if the outcome is not what we hope for, we conclude that our prayer is outside of His will. Is it possible that we didn't pray in confidence according *to* His will?

When it comes to healing, we can be assured of God's will. It's His nature to heal. A healthy body is God's plan for your life and a reflection of His goodness and His abundant love for you. He grieves over all human brokenness and wants you to be completely whole. Sickness and death were never part of His original plan. God created, called creation good, and gave humans dominion over the earth (Genesis 1; Psalm 8). Sickness and oppression are products of the fall, and when sin entered the world, all creation fell into decay (Genesis 3:7; Romans 8:21). But Jesus came to set these systems right again, to take back what the enemy stole from us. Through His death and resurrection, God provided the full measure of grace to restore all things (Colossians 1:20). He came to destroy the works of the devil (1 John 3:8). He healed you by the stripes on his back (Isaiah 53:5 NKJV).

If we pray "if it be Your will" prayers for healing, what we are really praying is "Lord, if it's not Your will to heal me, then let this sickness take me!" Does that sound like Jesus? Jesus healed everyone who came to Him. There are no Bible stories of people who came to Jesus and walked away without their healing, and no cases where He turned down a person's request for healing. In fact, there are many times when the Bible says He healed *all* who came to Him (Acts 10:38; Matthew 8:16; 12:15; 4:24; Luke 6:19). In fact, Jesus never prayed "if it be Your will" prayers for healing, and neither did His disciples. They directed their prayers at the condition and prayed with authority. They spoke commands like "Pick up your mat, and walk!" (John 5:8) or "Be cleansed" (Matthew 8:3 NKJV).

They didn't use "if it be Your will" prayers because they

knew God's will to heal. Remember, God planned for you to live a long, full, and satisfying life (Psalm 91:16; John 10:10). He promised to care for you throughout your lifetime—until your hair is white with age (Isaiah 46:4)! If God's heart is to heal and to give you a long life, then you can approach Him with confidence. He wants you well.

## Prayer

*Lord, thank You that You came to destroy the works of the devil, to take back what he stole in the garden. Forgive me when I doubt Your will to heal me, for believing the lie that this affliction came from Your hands. Thank You for providing the full measure of grace to heal and restore me through Your death and resurrection.*

*Please give me faith to believe I can pray for anything, and if I believe I've received it, it will be mine (Mark 11:24). Lord, I received my healing by the stripes on Your back (Isaiah 53:5 NKJV). When I pray, please give me faith to believe that healing is truly Your will for me. I am sorry for the times I have prayed "if it be Your will" prayers out of doubt and unbelief, rather than true reverence and dependence on You. Give me the faith to approach You in confidence, fully believing that You want me well.*

# He Does Not Change

*Jesus Christ is the same yesterday, today, and forever.*
HEBREWS 13:8

He was a pastor, a missionary who carried God's message of salvation through faith in Jesus Christ to the indigenous people in South America. One day he was summoned by a villager to come quickly to the bedside of a dying infant. The mother believed that Jesus could save her child. What she didn't know was that the missionary believed certain doctrines in the New Testament were things that applied only in the days of the Bible. He had been taught that God healed in the past, but not today, and that the gifts of the Spirit were only for believers in Bible times. He looked at the desperate mother, her eyes pleading for her child's life, and the impossible situation facing him. Not knowing what else to do, and knowing full well his unbelief, he prayed for Jesus to heal the child. Jesus did, and this pastor's ministry changed forever.

In His own ministry, Jesus didn't just explain through words alone that He had come to forgive people's sins and give them eternal life. He combined preaching about forgiveness, healing the sick, and expelling demons as a demonstration of the fullness of the Gospel and the goodness of God (Acts 10:36–38). He publicly announced His mission—to release the prisoners, recover sight for the blind, and set the oppressed free—at the synagogue in Nazareth when He announced He was the One appointed by God to fulfill Isaiah's prophecy (Luke 4:18–19). In His three-year ministry, He traveled throughout the region of Galilee, teaching in the synagogues and announcing the good news of the Kingdom and healing every kind of disease (Matthew 4:23).

But Jesus didn't stop there. He gave His disciples the power and authority to go out into the world and do the same things He was doing in His name (John 17:18). He started by sending the twelve disciples closest to Him. He gave them power and authority to cast out *all* demons, heal *all* diseases, and to tell everyone about the Kingdom (Luke 9:1–2). Next, He chose seventy-two other disciples and sent them out in pairs to all the towns He planned to visit, instructing them to do the same. They returned rejoicing because they saw the same results as Jesus (Luke 10:1–20). Finally, He gave the same mission to all believers through the Great Commission. He instructs us to "go into all the world and preach the Good News to everyone. Anyone who believes and is baptized will be saved. . . . These miraculous signs will accompany those who believe. . . . They will be able to place their hands on the sick, and they will be healed" (Mark 16:15–18).

After the religious leaders commanded Peter and John never to preach the name of Jesus again, the believers prayed together in boldness for the power to preach and heal (Acts 4:29–30). The Lord answered their prayer and they performed many healing miracles in His name (Acts 3:6–8; 5:16). In bringing God's message to the Gentiles, Paul said that they were convinced by the power of miraculous signs and wonders and by the power of God's Spirit. In this way, he said he had *fully* presented the good news of Christ (Romans 15:18–19).

Jesus wants to do everything through His people now that He did when He was here on the earth. He said anyone who believes in Him will do the same works He has done, and even greater works (John 14:12). Will you be like this woman with the sick child and take Jesus at His word? She needed more from this missionary than just hearing the message of salvation. She needed him to fully present the good news. She expected to experience the power of Jesus through him. Jesus healed then and He heals now. He does not change.

## Prayer

*Lord, forgive me for ever doubting that Your healing power is limited today. Lord, I thank You for the gift of eternal life. I want more than a Gospel of head knowledge and the promise of salvation. I want a Gospel of power. Holy Spirit, come! I want to know Your presence.*

*Jesus, You sent out the twelve and the seventy-two, and then You commissioned all believers to go make disciples and to lay hands on the sick and heal them in Your name. You work through the body of believers now, just like You healed through Your own body then. I believe You are still willing and able to heal my body, soul, and spirit in response to my faith in You. You are Jehovah-Rapha, the God who heals. And You do not change.*

## Jehovah-Rapha: Kevin's Story

He walked into the dimly lit chapel where the prayer meeting was being held. Candles flickered around the room and soft music played in the background. A kind woman greeted him and ushered him to a comfortable chair in the corner of the room. He followed her slowly, but he soon knew the soft armchair she indicated for him simply would not work. He noticed several portable straight-back chairs in the room. "I'll just sit in one of these," he said. "Can you help?"

"Of course." She smiled as she held his hands so he could carefully lower himself into the chair. "Someone will be with you shortly," she said, and then returned to her post at the door.

He watched her greet others coming into the room. A bald man with his family. A woman in a wheelchair being pushed by someone who was likely her son. Others filed in, all with cancer, he supposed. *Cancer.* His nemesis. For him, prostate cancer. He vowed to fight, but the disease proved itself relentless. The metastases in his spine were the final blow. The doctor said the neck brace might give his crumbling cervical spine some protection before it collapsed and paralyzed him. His lower back wasn't much better. He parked the motorcycle and everything else he enjoyed doing.

He was not really sure why he came here tonight, and he didn't really know what to expect. Maybe the cancer had finally forced him to accept his fate and to think about what might be next. He knew about heaven and why Jesus died. His Catholic upbringing had taught him that much. Maybe now he wanted to be sure. Maybe that was the comfort he was seeking—the assurance that when he took his last breath on earth, there would be something more and what the nuns said was true. Maybe it was to find some kind of spiritual relief from the pain that was intensifying every day as the cancer spread relentlessly throughout his body. Or maybe it was the fear of dying. *What will it be like? I'm not ready, God. No, I'm not ready.*

His thoughts were interrupted by the female pastor who pulled up a chair next to his. "Hello, Kevin. I'm so glad you came. I understand you're on quite a journey." *Not one I would choose.* They exchanged small talk. He filled her in on his condition and the gloomy prognosis. They talked about his faith background. "Have you invited Jesus into the middle of all this?" she asked. "I think so. Maybe not," Kevin answered. "Well, let's do that first," she said. "I'll lead you through some prayers."

After she prayed for him, he felt good. Her next question caught him off guard. "Kevin, do you believe the Lord can heal you?" *Heal me?* He was an engineer by training. A scientist. He focused on a reality he could see, hear, and manipulate. Things he could prove. It was difficult enough to acknowledge that God, an unseen, distant spiritual being, might be able to comfort him, let alone heal him. "No," he said flatly. "That would take a miracle, and I don't believe in miracles."

Over the next hour, they engaged in a spirited discussion on the biblical basis for healing. She pointed to the healing ministry of Jesus and how He had given others, including believers today, the mandate and authority to heal. "That was only to build up the church," he responded. She read James 5:14–15, where James told the sick to call for elders of the church to pray over them in faith and the Lord would make them well. "If that were true, then your prayers would heal everyone," he concluded, and then added, "Jesus suffered. Why shouldn't we?" She responded, "He suffered *for* you. By His stripes, you were healed." By the time the evening ended, she could see he really *wanted* to be convinced. He was intrigued, but he wanted proof. So she sent him home with a classic book by a Catholic priest who was a renowned biblical scholar on the subject of healing.

The book was compelling. So compelling, he couldn't put it down. He fought to stay awake, to keep reading, hoping this priest could change his mind. Hoping God could change his mind. He drifted in and out of sleep. There was a light on somewhere. In the kitchen? *I thought I turned all the lights off.* The light drew him out of bed. He followed it down the hall toward the kitchen, but the kitchen light was off. *Where is it coming from?* It continued to draw him, and he continued moving toward it. Finally he found himself in the screened-in porch with the Source of the light. With Jesus. *Am I dreaming?*

Jesus' arms were outstretched. Kevin walked right into them, directly into the light of His glorious presence. Into His rest. Into His peace. Never had he experienced a love like this. So perfect, so complete. *Forgive me, Lord. Cleanse me. Make me whole.* Layer upon layer began dropping off. A lifetime of lies replaced with truth about Father God, truth about himself. Painful wounds and memories bound and healed. Sin washed away, never to be remembered again. *Beautiful Savior. I'm free.*

He awoke in his bed that morning to sunlight streaming in through the windows. The Light was still there. It hovered over him like a glorious blanket, penetrating and warming the very core of his being. He left the neck brace at home that day. That afternoon, the doctor was stunned to find his PSA had dropped to near normal levels. A few days later, he learned his spine appeared to be regenerating. Soon after that, he got back on his motorcycle. His life had taken another unexpected turn. He was now on a journey to share God's hope and to tell the world that miracles really do happen.

# More Than Enough

*She replied, "That's true, Lord, but even dogs are allowed to eat*
*the scraps that fall beneath their masters' table." "Dear woman,"*
*Jesus said to her, "your faith is great. Your request is granted."*
*And her daughter was instantly healed.*
MATTHEW 15:27–28

She watched her little girl sitting in the corner on the
floor, cradling her knees and rocking back and forth. She
remembered the day she was born. She was so perfect. *How
did this happen?* She could no longer play with the other
children. Days of sulking and sadness could turn into fits of
rage in an instant. She would thrash on the floor, resisting all
help to calm and restrain her. On other occasions, she would
charge at others without cause or notice, and sometimes
inflict wounds on her own body. She could no longer keep
her safe.

She must find this Jesus. *Why would He come here?* Some
said He was escaping from the conflict with the Pharisees
and elders in His own country. He often withdrew to such
distant places. *But why here, why Tyre?* She was Greek by
birth, born in Syrian Phoenicia, and well aware of the ancient
rivalry between the Jews and Canaanites. There was a long
history of spiritual and military conflict between them. The
Jews thought the Canaanites were thoroughly pagan and
corrupt. Their presence in the land had been a strong threat
to the purity of Israel's religion and morality. *Why would this
Jewish rabbi come to Canaanite country?* No matter. He could
drive out the demon that tormented her little girl. She must
find Him.

Reaching the neighborhood where she heard He might be, she began searching for Him. "Have you seen Jesus?" she asked the shopkeepers, bystanders, and anyone who would listen. "Have you seen Him?" Someone nodded and pointed. Spotting Him with His disciples, she ran up to Him and fell at His feet. "Have mercy on me, O Lord, Son of David! For my daughter is possessed by a demon that torments her severely," she pleaded relentlessly.

Jesus looked at her and said nothing. The disciples appeared annoyed. "Tell her to go away. She is bothering us with all her begging." Jesus finally spoke. "I was sent only to help God's lost sheep—the people of Israel." She could not bear it. *No, I will not believe this Jewish Messiah has nothing left to help a desperate Canaanite mother.* She fell down and worshipped Him, pleading again, "Lord, help me!" Jesus responded, "It isn't right to take food from the children and throw it to the dogs." At that moment, she knew she had a decision to make. *Did this Jewish king just call me a dog?* A swirl of emotion threatened to rise up from within, but pure desperation pushed it back down. *No, I will not allow anything to stand in the way of my daughter getting well.* She responded calmly and resolutely, "That's true, Lord, but even dogs are allowed to eat the scraps that fall beneath their master's table." Jesus replied, "Dear woman, your faith is great. I have healed your daughter." *Thank You, Son of David. Thank You for mercy.* She returned home, and sure enough, she found her little girl lying quietly in bed. The demon was gone (Matthew 15:21–28; Mark 7:24–30).

Yes, Jesus called her a dog. The Jews commonly called the Canaanites dogs. He may have done so with disdain toward their attitudes and to show a contrast with His own. Or perhaps He was trying to teach the disciples that His first priority was to provide food for the children of Israel and not to let something like a family pet interrupt the meal. In essence, He was telling her that the Jews had the first opportunity to accept Him as Messiah and spread His message of salvation to the world (Genesis 12:3).

By calling Him "Son of David," she believed He was the promised Messiah. And if that were true, as a Jewish king He was sovereign over her and the land. Even though their conversation most likely opened old wounds, she was so desperate for her daughter to be healed that she was willing to cry out for mercy from the visiting Jewish king. She was willing to be called a dog, to be considered an interruption, and to take the scraps from His table in order for her daughter to be free. She worshipped Him and she pleaded. She refused to take offense, and in doing so, her heart was unblocked. Jesus used the situation to show that faith was for all people, Jew or Gentile. He responded to her faith and humility by healing her daughter. Ironically, this Gentile woman and others like her received from Jesus what many Jews would miss—the salvation first intended for them.

Sometimes we take offense over what God appears to be doing or not doing without having the full picture. Maybe today you're harboring grudges over old conflicts and hurts, and when a similar situation arises again, it opens up old wounds. God wants to unblock your heart. He doesn't want offense standing between you and your path to wholeness. When life seems unfair or doesn't make sense, even His leftovers are more than enough.

# Prayer

*Lord, sometimes I just don't understand Your ways. You appear to show favor to those who don't deserve it and withhold blessing from those who do. Please forgive me for taking offense when my wounds run deep and I don't have the full picture. Lord, please heal my wounds from past conflicts, relationships, and the attitudes of others. Help me to forgive those who have dishonored me, held me in contempt, or shown prejudice against me.*

*Thank You that You are the perfect Father. You are always fair and just. Have mercy on me, O Lord, Son of David! I worship You! Unblock my heart. I want to be unoffendable. I want nothing to stand in the way of my healing and wholeness. I am grateful, Lord. Even Your leftovers are more than enough.*

# Come to Jesus

*Then Jesus told them, "A prophet is honored everywhere except in his own hometown and among his relatives and his own family." And because of their unbelief, he couldn't do any miracles among them except to place his hands on a few sick people and heal them.*

MARK 6:4–5

It was the Sabbath, and a group huddled together in the synagogue waiting for Jesus to preach. He had returned to His hometown with His disciples from Capernaum, His base of operations. While waiting, they chatted about the things of daily life—the lack of rain, the new grandchild to be born any day now, the illness of a family member, the death of a friend, the wedding they would all be attending—typical small-town chatter. The service started and they waited for Jesus to speak. After all, He was one of their own. His rising-star status made them feel good about themselves and their town. Maybe knowing Him could even help them politically in the future.

They settled in to listen. At first they were astonished. "Where did He get all this wisdom and the power to perform such miracles?" one of them whispered. But as Jesus continued to preach, they became increasingly offended. "He's just a carpenter, the son of Mary and the brother of James, Joseph, Judas, and Simon. And His sisters live right here among us. What makes Him so great?" The murmurs continued throughout the village. *His mother is so quiet. If He was something special, God's Promise to Israel, wouldn't she have told us? She never said a word about this. He and His father did some work for us. He was kind, polite, and hardworking, but nothing special. I've known their family for years. They are common Jews just like us. Who does He think He is anyway?* They were deeply offended that others could be impressed enough to follow Him and refused to believe in Him.

Echoes of this conversation play out in communities everywhere. Small-town kid makes it big. A high school sports star makes the pros. The lead in the high school play becomes a big-time box office name. The church choir soloist signs with a major label. But Jesus was not just any small-town boy.

Over three hundred prophecies spanning a thousand years promised that the Messiah would come and save Israel from their oppression. And they were expected to believe that this hometown boy, the son of a carpenter, a playmate of their own children, was the promised Hope of Israel? It was difficult enough to believe He would establish an earthly kingdom and reign as King of the Jews. But now they were supposed to accept Him as equal to the God of Israel, having the same power as He to forgive their sins? A man they should worship in the same way they worshipped their Father in heaven? No, it was too much (Mark 6:1–6).

Jesus was teaching in their synagogue, but unlike the other places He visited, He could do few miracles in His own hometown. Very few people were saved and healed. It was not possible that the Creator of the universe suddenly lost His power to heal through His Son. Maybe it was their lack of faith that blocked their blessing, or perhaps He chose not to heal because of their pride and unbelief. Or quite possibly, He healed a few because only a few came to Him. They thought they knew Him, but their preconceived notions made it impossible to accept His message and receive His miracles because they didn't believe He was from God. They rejected

His authority and took offense. Their pride blinded them to who He was. They simply couldn't see beyond the man. *And He was one of them.* Amazed by their unbelief, Jesus looked elsewhere for those who would respond.

If pride is keeping you from responding to Jesus, it's time to let it go. If unbelief is robbing you of hope, it's time to let it go. If you have any doubt that He is God's Son and that by His Spirit He has the power and authority to save and heal—it's time to let it go. It's time to come to Jesus.

## Prayer

*Lord, help my unbelief. Please don't let it blind me to Your truth and steal my hope. Show me where I am holding on to pride, offense, doubt, or misconceptions that might cause me to miss out on all You have for me. Forgive me, Lord, if I have not truly known You. Help me to see beyond the man, beyond the good things You said and did. I want to know You as the Son of God, my personal Savior, Healer, Deliverer, and Friend. All authority in heaven and on earth has been given to You (Matthew 28:18). You are the only Way.*

*I come to You, Jesus. Do a mighty work in my life. I come for Your grace, Your mercy, and Your healing touch. Give me eyes to see and a heart to receive. I come to You.*

# Ordinary People

*As a result of the apostles' work, sick people were brought out into the streets on beds and mats so that Peter's shadow might fall across some of them as he went by. Crowds came from the villages around Jerusalem, bringing their sick and those possessed by evil spirits, and they were all healed.*
ACTS 5:15–16

The sick man looked around at the others, hundreds of people just like him, lying on their beds and mats in the street. They heard that the apostles had been performing many miraculous signs and wonders among the people, and they had all come to be healed. These apostles were just ordinary people. Jesus spent most of His time teaching and preparing them to carry out His ministry. He seemed to know His time here would be limited. They had all scattered on that dismal day when He was crucified, but there were reports that He had appeared to them several times during the forty days before He ascended into heaven. It was during these visits that He instructed them to go and do what He had been doing (John 20:21): to make more disciples (Matthew 28:19), to preach the good news, and to lay hands on sick people to make them well (Mark 16:15, 18).

People said they had waited in Jerusalem to receive His power for seven long weeks (Acts 1:4). When the Holy Spirit finally came upon them at Pentecost, the apostle Peter gave a courageous speech that compelled three thousand more people to join their cause (Acts 2:41). Even after the religious leaders warned them never to speak or preach the name of Jesus again, the believers prayed for boldness, and God sent His healing power so they could do miraculous signs and wonders in His name (Acts 4:30). They met regularly at Solomon's Colonnade on the east side of the temple where the apostles continued to preach and perform signs and wonders, in spite of the warning.

This morning, this sick man was among the latest crowd who hoped the apostles would be able to free them from the infirmities that held them captive in their beds. The size of the crowd was daunting; there were so many sick people from the villages all around Jerusalem, all desperate to be made whole. *Is it possible for the apostles to touch and heal all of us?*

At that moment, he noticed someone stepping through the mats and beds that cluttered the street. *Is it Peter?* The sun was at his back, casting a shadow in front of him. The sick man blinked, not quite believing his eyes. It looked as though people were jumping up from their sickbeds as soon as they were touched by Peter's shadow! *Can this be happening?*

Soon, Peter's shadow reached him, too, and he felt power rush through his body. Before he could comprehend the miracle, he was standing with the crowd, their mats and beds forgotten, praising the Lord. He was healed. The sickness that had ravaged his body was completely gone. Others had received their sight, had their ears unplugged, and had various diseases healed. Still others stood on legs that were no longer crippled and had demons dispelled. As he looked around, he realized they were *all* healed. Every single one.

Jesus gave His apostles the power to do miracles, preach boldly, and carry His presence into the world. The religious leaders were amazed, for they could see that they were ordinary men with no special training except that they had been with Jesus (Acts 4:13). As a result, they were able to confirm the truth of their teaching, attract new believers to the early church, and demonstrate that the power of Jesus was now with them. The apostles never saw Jesus refuse to heal a sick person. They simply followed His teaching and all were healed.

God is still working mightily in His church today, and our mandate hasn't changed. We are to proclaim the good news of the Kingdom with the same boldness and expectancy as the apostles did. Jesus demonstrated His power through ordinary people who were obedient to His call and relentlessly pursued an intimate relationship with the living God. Through them, He didn't heal a few. He didn't heal some. He healed them all.

## Prayer

*Praise You, Lord, for making disciples out of ordinary people in order to take Your message of hope into the world. Thank You for trusting all of us to continue doing what You did (John 20:21), to preach the good news to everyone everywhere (Mark 16:15), to lay hands on the sick and make them well (Mark 16:18), to make disciples of all nations (Matthew 28:19), and to be Your witnesses to the ends of the earth (Acts 1:8).*

*Breathe on me, Lord. I receive Your Spirit. I may have no special training, but I carry Your power. Help me to believe and proclaim the Gospel with the same boldness, fervency, and expectancy as the apostles. Help me to always remember that You didn't just heal some. You healed them all.*

# The Secret Place

*Because you have made the LORD, who is my refuge,
even the Most High, your dwelling place, no evil shall befall you,
nor shall any plague come near your dwelling.*
PSALM 91:9–10 NKJV

Scholars believe King David is most likely the author of Psalm 91. He certainly needed a secret place. When King Saul deliberately disobeyed God, He instructed the prophet Samuel to anoint David as Saul's replacement. David quickly killed Goliath and then became lifelong friends with Saul's son Jonathan. King Saul was so pleased with David's musical talent and military successes that he took David into his home and treated him as a son. But he soon realized David would become king, and his insane jealousy drove him into a murderous rage. David and his loyal followers fled for their lives to the hills with Saul and his army in relentless pursuit. They hid in the caves in Philistine territory for many years before Saul died and David finally became king of Judah in his place.

In Psalm 91, David refers to his secret place as "the shadow," "my refuge," "my place of safety," "shelter," and "dwelling." In Psalm 31:20 (NKJV), he directly refers to being hidden "in the secret place of Your presence" and being kept "secretly in a pavilion." Other psalms also describe this secret place:

- "For you are my hiding place; you protect me from trouble. You surround me with songs of victory (Psalm 32:7)."

- "How precious is your unfailing love, O God! All humanity finds shelter in the shadow of your wings" (Psalm 36:7).
- "The LORD rescues the godly; he is their fortress in times of trouble. The LORD helps them, rescuing them from the wicked. He saves them, and they find shelter in him" (Psalm 37:39–40).
- "Have mercy on me, O God, have mercy! I look to you for protection. I will hide beneath the shadow of your wings until the danger passes by" (Psalm 57:1).
- "Lead me to the towering rock of safety, for you are my safe refuge, a fortress where my enemies cannot reach me. Let me live forever in your sanctuary, safe beneath the shelter of your wings!" (Psalm 61:2–4).

For most Israelites in the Old Testament, God's presence was in the Holy of Holies, a sacred place in the temple that only priests could access in their behalf. But Jesus came to make the secret place of God's presence accessible to all believers. When He announced that "the Kingdom of God is near," He made it clear that He was the long-awaited Messiah who had come to break the power of sin and death (Mark 1:15). When we accept Him as our Lord and Savior, we are His temple and His presence lives in our hearts (1 Corinthians 6:19).

Yes, disease and sickness still exist in the world. Jesus said we will have many trials and sorrows on earth, but to take heart, because He has overcome the world (John 16:33). Until He returns, He gave us the Holy Spirit as a foretaste of the future when God will completely free the world of all sin, sickness, and evil (Romans 8:19–23).

In the meantime, He is with you. You can hide in His presence until the violent storms pass. He promises shelter and refuge in your times of trouble (Psalm 9:9). In His presence, you will find protection from harm, courage to face your fears, and rest for your soul. Make the Most High your dwelling place, and no evil will befall you; no plague will come near your dwelling. Meet Him now in the secret place.

## Prayer

*Lord, thank You for the promise of Your presence and for protecting me in the secret place where no plague can reach me. Please keep me safe beneath the shadow of Your wings. I pray each verse of Psalm 91(NKJV) as a confession of my faith in the power of Your covering:*

1. *I dwell in the secret place of the Most High so I abide under the shadow of the Almighty.*
2. *I will say of the LORD, "He is my refuge and my fortress; my God, in Him I will trust."*
3. *Surely He shall deliver me from the snare of the fowler and from the perilous pestilence.*
4. *He shall cover me with His feathers, and under His wings I shall take refuge; His truth shall be my shield and buckler.*
5. *I shall not be afraid of the terror by night, nor of the arrow that flies by day.*
6. *I shall not be afraid of the pestilence that walks in darkness, nor of the destruction that lays waste at noonday.*
7. *A thousand may fall at my side, and ten thousand at my right hand; but it shall not come near me.*

8. *Only with my eyes shall I look, and see the reward of the wicked.*

9. *Because I have made the L*ORD*, who is my refuge, even the Most High, my dwelling place,*

10. *No evil shall befall me, nor shall any plague come near my dwelling;*

11. *For He shall give His angels charge over me, to keep me in all my ways.*

12. *They shall bear me up in their hands, lest I dash my foot against a stone.*

13. *I shall tread upon the lion and the cobra, the young lion and the serpent I shall trample underfoot.*

14. *Because I have set my love upon Him, therefore He will deliver me; He will set me on high, because I have known His name.*

15. *I shall call upon Him, and He will answer me; He will be with me in trouble; He will deliver me and honor me.*

16. *With long life He will satisfy me, and show me His salvation.*

# Save Me, Lord!

*Then Peter called to him, "Lord, if it's really you, tell me to come to you, walking on the water." "Yes, come," Jesus said. So Peter went over the side of the boat and walked on the water toward Jesus. But when he saw the strong wind and the waves, he was terrified and began to sink. "Save me, Lord!" he shouted.*
MATTHEW 14:28–30

Peter stared into the blackness, pondering what he had just witnessed. The crowds had followed them to a town called Bethsaida where Jesus was seeking solitude after hearing about the death of John the Baptist. In spite of His grief, He preached and healed many. Then, instead of sending them away when they became hungry, He fed five thousand men, plus women and children, with five loaves of bread and two fish and had twelve baskets of leftovers! When the crowds finally left, Peter and the disciples left Jesus behind on the mountainside to pray while they hopped on a boat back to the other side.

Peter's thoughts were suddenly interrupted by a roaring wind that rose while they were far from land in the middle of the lake. As a fisherman, he was familiar with these squalls, but this one was fierce. Shouting orders at each other, they struggled desperately to row against the heavy waves that crashed over the sides of the boat. Fighting to keep the boat from sinking, Peter caught sight of something moving in the blackness. A figure was coming toward them, gliding slowly over the top of the water. He blinked, thinking it must be his imagination. "Look!" he screamed in terror, forgetting the storm and the sinking boat. "It's a ghost!"

Calmly and gently, the figure spoke. Peter immediately recognized the voice. "It's all right," Jesus said. "I am here! Don't be afraid." *It is the Lord!* Peter immediately called out to Him, "Lord, if it's really You, tell me to come to You by walking on the water."

"All right, come," Jesus said. Without hesitation, Peter jumped over the side of the boat. His eyes locked onto Jesus' eyes. They were one, and nothing else mattered. Nothing else existed. And then he realized what was really happening. *I'm walking on the water's surface in the middle of the lake, and I'm not sinking!* Stunned, he took his eyes off Jesus for just a second and noticed the high waves crashing around him. Suddenly, he was terrified and began to sink. "Save me, Lord!" he shouted. Instantly, Jesus reached out His hand and grabbed him (Matthew 14:1–36).

Peter was so faith-filled and connected to Jesus that he even shared Jesus' power over the natural realm. He only panicked and sank because he took his eyes off the Lord and focused on his circumstances. He began depending on his own strength and became aware of his own limitations.

When we battle sickness, we can easily focus on our symptoms, doctors, tests, medications, and prognoses. We take our eyes off Jesus, the ultimate Healer and the only One who can calm the storm. We shouldn't put our heads in the sand and deny what's happening around us, but we do have to remember that the facts are temporal and worldly, while God's truth is eternal and His power is unlimited. Yes, you may be sick, but the truth is you have been healed by His wounds (1 Peter 2:24). Your illness may be very serious, but nothing is impossible with God (Luke 1:37). God's Word is always true whether we experience it on this earth or not. In His power, it's possible to transcend the facts like Peter did. In His presence, peace reigns instead of fear when the storms rage around you.

In spite of witnessing the miracle of Jesus feeding the five thousand  earlier and the faith he had found to walk on water, Peter still panicked and sank. Jesus pulled him out of the water and immediately calmed the storm. Likewise, even though we may know His power is unlimited, we can lose our focus and quickly sink into a lake of fear and despair. But it is impossible for Him to let you drown. His death proved His unconquerable love. Despite your circumstances, overwhelming victory is always yours. His eternal truth always triumphs over the facts. He knows when your faith is strong enough for you to walk on water. And when you sink into the bottom of the lake, He hears your cries: "Save me, Lord!"

## Prayer

*Thank You, Lord, that in You I have access to the same power that raised You from the dead and conquered natural law so Peter could walk on the water. Forgive me when I lose my focus and let the storms of life pull my eyes off You. Forgive me when I depend on my own strength instead of Yours and forget that Your power has no limits.*

*Thank You for hearing my cries when I start to sink to the bottom of the lake! Lord, You are the only One who can calm the storm, and the only One with the power to save. I know Your perfect love is enough to conquer all my fears. Lord, calm the storm around me. Calm the storm in my heart. Help me keep my eyes firmly planted on You and Your truth when the high waves crash around me. Please, Lord! Give me the faith to walk on water. Help me to stand firm in Your presence. I receive Your peace.*

# Jehovah-Rapha: Ryan's Story

The first symptoms were insidious. Preseason football practice was under way for the small Christian college he attended. He tried to ignore the symptoms at first. It took all the effort he could muster to move his arms and legs through the practice drills. He chalked up the lack of energy and joint pain to being out of shape and therefore not prepared for the rigorous practices like he should have been. The intermittent fever? He must be fighting off a bug. He was always fighting some sort of bug. Then the night sweats started, and he realized he had lost his appetite and was dropping weight. Not a good way to start out his senior season as the team punter. If he didn't step it up, he might even lose his spot to one of the lowerclassmen.

The team doctor noticed and had some concerns about his preseason physical. It was time to see a specialist for more tests. They prodded and poked and drew blood and tissue samples. And now the results were in. He fidgeted in his chair in the exam room, with his mother next to him flipping through a magazine. She had been concerned for quite a while and kept telling him he needed to get things checked out. Her mother antenna was sounding the alarm. Now, he knew her nonchalance and apparent lack of concern were all for his benefit. She didn't want to worry him, and neither one wanted to talk about the diagnosis they knew the doctors suspected.

When the doctor entered the room, Ryan searched his face for some clue that he might have positive news. So much for hope. The doctor's face was grim and serious. "I'm sorry, Ryan. The tests confirmed our suspicions. You have leukemia." From that point on, the conversation turned surreal. Fighting back tears, his mother fired off a list of questions. She had done her research. *Are you sure? How bad is it? What treatment do you recommend? What are the side effects? What does it involve? Does it work? What are his chances of beating this?* The doctor's words were muffled and distant, as if he were listening from underwater. He stared at the door and was tempted to get up and leave. He wanted to get to his car and drive as far away as he could to escape this life-shattering news.

The treatment would be extensive, with long hospital stays necessary for the chemotherapy. There would be side effects, likely severe. But there was good news. He was young. The younger the better when battling a disease like acute leukemia. They weren't kidding about the side effects. They were brutal. He was dizzy, weak, bald, and miserable. The entire inside of his mouth was covered with sores. When he was able to get something through the pain and into his stomach, it went right through him. Nurses were constantly tending to his IVs, giving him medications, taking his vitals, and helping him to the bathroom. Doctors hovered in the corner with his family speaking in hushed tones. He had vague memories of a steady stream of friends who came to visit. Some joked around and treated him as if everything was normal. Others were clearly uncomfortable and stumbled to say the right thing. Still others prayed. Weeks turned to months in and out of the hospital. He felt the treatment would never end. Finally, it did. The blood work looked promising. More tests confirmed it. There were no more signs of cancer. He was home free, or at least "in remission."

Recovery took way longer than he anticipated. He had missed his senior year and then some. Football was a distant memory. Without a job, he had to move in with his mother. He was not mentally ready to handle coursework, and his medical condition complicated his insurance options. He felt stuck, like his life had been put in an unfair holding pattern. He was going in for checkups and being closely monitored by his doctors. Time passed and the fog began to lift. Life was feeling somewhat normal again. He started to make plans and to think about the future. He was ready to go back to finish school when the news came. The cancer was back.

This time it was more serious. He would need a bone marrow transplant. They would have to find a donor who matched, hopefully a family member. The high-dose chemotherapy they would use to destroy the existing cancer and bone marrow cells would wipe out his entire immune system and make his previous treatments pale in comparison. He was back in the same cancer center. The same hospital floor. The same doctors and nurses. Only this time was different. This time, he was done. It was too much. Darkness overwhelmed him. He would no longer fight this.

The parents of a close friend came to visit that night. She was a cancer survivor. They both loved the Lord and believed He had both the compassion and power to heal Ryan. They came to pray. "You can pray if you want," Ryan said. "But you need to know, I'm ready to go. I'm done fighting." The couple began to pray. They prayed for the Father to release His love over Ryan, that he would know his identity and value as a son of God. They rebuked the cancer and commanded it to leave in the mighty name of Jesus. They read and declared healing scriptures over him and prayed for courage, peace, and protection. Tears rolled down his cheeks and he could feel the presence of the Holy Spirit in the room.

Others came to pray over the next several days. Family and friends pressed in, seeking the Lord around the clock. Ryan's will to live began to return. Prayers were answered when a younger brother tested as a perfect donor match. The conditioning process to prepare for the transplant was indeed brutal, but God's grace carried him through. The transplant procedure itself went well, but it took him months to regain his strength and ensure his body wouldn't reject the transplant. With each test and each visit, the doctors grew more encouraged. Gradually, Ryan began to feel whole again. God was restoring more than his physical health. He was healing him from the inside out, bringing his body, soul, and spirit into alignment. He was giving him a new life in Christ.

Ryan's life was forever changed. In his darkest hour, when he had lost all hope, when he couldn't pray, God sent people who could. He was overwhelmed with gratitude at the goodness of God and His mercy. He was humbled by the presence of Jesus he felt through the love and compassion of his family and friends. During this time of recovery and reflection, he began to feel a tug in the deepest,  innermost places of his spirit. A sacred call to serve the Lord that few are privileged to receive.

Ryan was obedient to the call. After completing four robust years of seminary, he received his first call to serve as lead pastor. There wasn't a dry eye at his ordination service, or at his wedding a few months later. Today he marvels at how the Lord redeemed everything the enemy intended for evil in his life and turned it into something beautiful. But he is not surprised. Because he knows God is good. He is love. He is Jehovah-Rapha, the God who heals.

# Because of Your Faith

*They went right into the house where he was staying, and Jesus asked them,*
*"Do you believe I can make you see?" "Yes, Lord," they told him, "we do."*
*Then he touched their eyes and said, "Because of your faith, it will happen."*
MATTHEW 9:28–29

The two blind men were as determined as ever after what they had just witnessed. This man they called Jesus had just raised the daughter of their local synagogue leader from the dead! He had insisted she was only asleep to the mocking crowd. Then He walked right into her room and took the girl by the hand, and she stood up (Matthew 9:24–26)! Surely, this Jesus must be the promised Messiah. Who else could raise the dead? Now it was their turn. Long ago, Isaiah prophesied that He would come and bring sight to the blind (Isaiah 29:18; 35:5; 42:7). And they were both as blind as could be. Surely He would heal them, too.

Following Him from the home of the resurrected girl, the two blind men shouted, "Son of David, have mercy on us!" They knew the Messiah would come from the house of David, and they wanted to address Him properly (Isaiah 9:7). Without waiting for an invitation, they barged right into the house where He was staying, nearly stepping on His heels.

Jesus turned to face them. He looked at them intently before He finally spoke. "Do you believe I can make you see?" They both shouted, "Yes, Lord, we do!" He paused again while they both stood in eager anticipation of what He was going to do. Neither one had any doubt in their mind that their sight would be restored. After all, they were standing in the presence of the Anointed One. Surely He would touch their eyes or say the words, and their lives would be forever changed. They were almost giddy with excitement. All the hopes and dreams they had shared about having their sight restored would soon become reality. They would no longer beg. They would work for an honest living. Perhaps they would even marry!

When enough silence had passed, He touched their eyes and said, "Because of your faith, it will happen." Immediately, their eyes were opened! The first sight they beheld was the beautiful face of the Savior. Even though He sternly warned them not to tell anyone, they ran out the door telling everyone who would listen what the Lord had done for them (Mathew 9:23–31).

Not everyone who asks for or receives prayer for healing *really* believes God can do it. Jesus may have paused just to see how faith-filled they really were. What He discovered was two persistent men who knew the Lord could heal them. They were determined not to let anything stop them from receiving what they knew He could do. His hesitation didn't rattle them. His silence didn't cause them to doubt or shrink back. They just waited confidently, knowing He would act when He was ready. It never crossed their minds to think He might not restore their sight. They believed the scriptures. They believed He was the Messiah.

There are many instances in the Bible where Jesus rewarded people for their faith—either the person needing healing or someone on their behalf. The writer of Hebrews says it is impossible to please God without faith (Hebrews 11:6). Does this mean, then, that He can't or won't heal you if you don't have "enough faith"? Absolutely not. He is God, and He won't let human reasoning define Him or put Him into a predictable box. If you need more faith, ask Him. Spend time in His presence, and let the Holy Spirit work. Be healed *because* of your faith.

## Prayer

*Lord, I want faith like these two blind men, a confident, persistent faith that makes no room for doubt and is not moved by Your silence, Your delays, or my own impatience. Like Your apostles before me, I ask You to increase my faith (Luke 17:5). You said it only takes faith as small as a mustard seed to move a mountain (Matthew 17:20). Lord, please give me enough faith to move my mountain! I believe nothing is impossible for You! I pray expectantly, knowing You are the Messiah, the living God who heals.*

*Lord, in times of silence when it doesn't feel like You are moving, protect me from the lies of the enemy, lies that would tell me you don't care or have forgotten about me. Lord, let nothing stop me from receiving my healing! Help me not to shrink back in doubt. Because of my faith, may it happen.*

# Just Ask

*Yet you don't have what you want because you don't ask God for it.*
JAMES 4:2

The service ends and the double doors to the prayer room swing wide to receive anyone needing prayer. The two prayer team leaders stand by the door greeting people who file past to reach the main exit. The large suburban megachurch hosts thousands of worshippers on a typical weekend, and trained prayer ministers are always available to pray for anyone who is sick, hurting, or struggling with difficulties. The leaders warmly greet those who come through the doors seeking prayer and direct them to the appropriate prayer ministers.

Most people simply pass by. One man pulls his oxygen tank on wheels. Another woman limps past struggling with her crutches. A couple of wheelchairs roll past with loved ones pushing behind. Some peer inside curiously but keep on walking. Still others pass by with glum faces, avoiding eye contact with the prayer leaders. Only God knows the depth of their personal pain or physical ailments. Maybe some are already receiving prayer support from a pastor or their small groups. Perhaps they prefer to take their prayer needs to the Lord privately. Is it possible that the majority have problem-free lives with no real prayer needs? Not likely. The leaders wonder how many unmet needs pass by the door, simply because no one asks.

Many needs go unmet because people simply don't bring their requests to God in prayer. Sometimes pride is a factor. *I can work this out myself. Prayer is for desperate people, and I'm not desperate enough yet. I'll pray as a last resort. Besides, I don't want to bother God or anyone else with my problems. And I sure don't want to share my problems with perfect strangers. It's simply none of their business.* But Jesus said people are blessed when they realize their need for God and their total dependence on Him (Matthew 5:3). These people understand they can do nothing apart from His power (John 15:5). They know and have experienced God's power through the prayers of His people.

Still others feel unworthy. Dear one, Jesus spilled His blood to make you worthy! In the Old Testament, people could access God and His mercy only through the priests and their sacrifices. But Jesus became the ultimate sacrifice. His death and resurrection made it possible for you to have direct access to God through prayer. The writer of Hebrews said you can now come boldly to the throne of your gracious God where you will receive His mercy and find grace to help you when you need it most (Hebrews 4:16). He doesn't say come meekly. He says to come reverently and with bold assurance, because He loves you. You are worthy.

Even so, fear keeps many from accepting the invitation to come boldly to God through prayer. They may be uncomfortable allowing others to pray out loud for them. They don't know what to expect or what God might do. Maybe they have seen "faith healers" on television and the people they pray for do strange things, and they are afraid of losing control. Or perhaps they fear if they pray and lay everything on the line, God won't answer. Have you ever prayed for something very important in your life, and your prayers weren't answered in the way you had hoped or expected? If so, you might feel God let you down, and you can no longer trust Him with the deepest prayers of your heart.

We should never give up after a few halfhearted attempts

at prayer and conclude He doesn't answer, He doesn't hear, or He simply doesn't care. Jesus said that everyone who asks, receives. And everyone who seeks, finds (Matthew 7:8). We can have confidence that if we pray according to God's will, we will receive what we ask for (1 John 5:14). The more time we spend in His Word and conversing with Him in prayer, the more we get to know His heart and His character. The more we know God, the more our prayers align with His. Seek to know Him. Be persistent. Be bold. And then, just ask.

## Prayer

*Lord, forgive me for when I have withheld my prayers from You out of pride or fear. I am completely dependent on You for all my needs. I can do nothing apart from Your power. Lord, I am humbled that You loved me so much that You died to make me worthy. Thank You that I can come boldly into Your throne room and receive Your grace and mercy.*

*Lord, I come boldly before You now. I stand on holy ground, bought and paid for by Your blood. I will not shrink back in fear. Thank You that I can receive what I ask for when I pray in accordance with Your will. Your Word says Your will is to heal and restore. Heal me, Lord. Restore my health. Have mercy on me. I receive health and wholeness.*

# I Can't

*When Jesus saw him and knew he had been ill for a long time, he asked him,
"Would you like to get well?" "I can't, sir," the sick man said, "for I have no one
to put me into the pool when the water bubbles up. Someone else always gets
there ahead of me." Jesus told him, "Stand up, pick up your mat, and walk!"*
JOHN 5:6–8

He lay in his usual place by the pool of Bethesda along with crowds of miserable people just like him. Their sick bodies were strewn around the porches, each clamoring for a place in the shade under the colonnade roofs. Some were blind or disfigured. Many limped. Some were paralyzed just like him. When they weren't distracted by grumbling over whose plight was worse, they watched the pool with their eyes peeled, hoping to see some bubbles near the center. Some in Jerusalem believed that the Lord would occasionally send an angel to dip its wings in the pool, and the first one to get into the water when it was stirred would be healed. But it never really happened. The most desperate ones like him seldom made it into the water first. Only the most able-bodied among them had a chance to win the competition. When they came out, they felt better. A little, anyway.

After thirty-eight years, he had grown very used to this routine. He was an old-timer, with weather-worn skin and long, tangled gray hair to prove it. He had a certain reputation at the pool. He had his spot in the shade, and no one dared fight him for it. Years ago when he lost the use of his legs, he had begged God to heal him. But his prayers fell on deaf ears. He gave up on praying a long time ago. His limp legs hurt constantly, but they still refused to move. Sometimes he thought if his legs were so useless, then he shouldn't be able to feel them, either. Wishful thinking. All he had left was his life at the pool—long and boring days of waiting for the water to stir and grumbling with the others. And begging, of course.

And today was a good day for begging. It was the Sabbath feast and the people who passed by would occasionally throw a few coins their way. In the early afternoon, he spotted Him. A man he hadn't seen before. He seemed to have a following. There were murmurs among his sick friends. A teacher, some speculated. The Teacher was surveying all those waiting to jump into the pool when His eyes stopped and locked onto the paralyzed man's. The Teacher approached, and the man thought he might have pity and give him something.

Instead, the Teacher looked directly at him and asked, "Would you like to get well?" *What? I gave up on that a long time ago. Can't you see how old I am? There's no way an old guy like me can beat all these people into the pool. It never stirs anyway!* Instead of answering with the obvious, he said: "I can't, sir, for I have no one to put me into the pool when the water bubbles up. Someone else always gets there ahead of me." The Teacher looked intently at him. *Those eyes. Can He read my mind?* He had to look down. The Teacher finally said, "Stand up, pick up your mat, and walk!" Instantly, his legs began to tingle and twitch. He wiggled his toes and bent his knees. His legs came alive and he leapt off the mat! The pain was gone. He could walk! He could jump! "I'm healed! I can walk!" he shouted. The crowd became delirious. How had they missed it? "When did the water stir?" they all shouted at once. Not waiting around to explain, the man quickly rolled up his sleeping mat and scurried away on his new legs (John 5:1–13).

Hopelessness had been a way of life for this man. No one helped him, he had no hope of ever being helped, and he had lost hope in helping himself. Instead of responding with a resounding "Yes!" when Jesus asked if he wanted to get well, he focused on his circumstances, the pool, and all his limitations. There was no one to help him get in. Someone always got there first. Jesus knew, after thirty-eight long years, the man had grown content in his hopelessness.

You can always focus on how bad things look and all the reasons your situation seems bleak. *The drugs don't work. The doctors can't help me. It's always been this way. Nothing ever changes.* Or you can refuse to let your desperate circumstances destroy your hope. You can refuse to allow yourself to become content in your depression. No matter how hopeless things seem, God can reach places no human solution can touch. If you have Jesus, you always have hope. He can walk into your life anytime and ask, "Child, do you want to get well?" Nothing is impossible for Him. When you are tempted to say "I can't," remember *He* can.

## Prayer

*Lord, forgive me when I have settled for my circumstances. Forgive me for letting the world know how big my problems are, while forgetting how big YOU are. Help me never to grow complacent and give up my hope for wholeness and wellness. Even in the most hopeless circumstances when the world says no, You can say yes. You can restore all that appears lost. You can do what no doctor can do, and what modern medicine would call impossible. You can do for me what I can't do for myself.*

*Jesus, You spoke words of life to this hopeless man and immediately he was healed and restored. Speak those same words to me, Lord. I am ready. Lord, I want to get well!*

# Taste and See

*Taste and see that the LORD is good.*
*Oh, the joys of those who take refuge in him!*
PSALM 34:8

Imagine you have been invited to a dinner party. You are excited by this invitation because you love the host and all those included on the guest list, plus the host hinted that the menu will be especially delectable. The night finally arrives and you ring the doorbell, hungry and excited about the evening ahead. The host answers with a warm greeting. After some small talk with the other guests, he escorts you all into the dining room. The table is exquisitely set, and by the looks of each place setting, it will likely be a multicourse meal. By now, you are famished. After seating everyone and saying a dinner blessing, the host passes out a recipe card. "Here is our first course," he proudly states. As he reads through the list of ingredients and preparation methods, everyone makes approving comments. Some even suggest ways to improve on the dish. After quite some time, he passes out a recipe for the second course. The process repeats. Before you know it, the night is completely over, and the guests have reviewed and thoroughly discussed the recipes for each course. But no one has tasted a single morsel of food. The host stands up and thanks you for coming, and everyone graciously makes their way to the door.

Would you enjoy this dinner party? Probably not. Yet this is often how we experience our spiritual meals. We can cram a lifetime of knowledge about God, Jesus, and the Bible into our heads, sort of like the recipes at a dinner party. But do we really know *Him*? Have we tasted the food? Is it good? Scripture makes it clear that God's deepest desire for us is to know Him and to continually grow in our knowledge of Him (Ephesians 1:17–18). Paul counted everything else as garbage in comparison to knowing Jesus (Philippians 3:8). In the midst of losing everything and suffering excruciating physical pain, Job decided he would rather know God than to know the reason he suffered (Job 42:5–6). Peter concluded that when we know Him, we have everything we need (2 Peter 1:2–3).

From the very beginning, God planned for us to know Him. We were created to be in a personal relationship with the Creator of the universe! The Lord walked with Adam and Eve in paradise until their disobedience allowed sin to enter the world and He banished them from His presence. From that point on, generations of people repeatedly turned their hearts away from God to follow their sinful nature, even though He extended mercy countless times. He was so committed to restoring what Satan stole in the garden that He sent His Son to make things right. Jesus not only came to heal the sick and set the captives free (Luke 4:18); He came to live once again in relationship with us. This relationship doesn't start when our mortal bodies die and we enter eternal life. We can be saved but relationally distant. We can have "head" knowledge without "heart" knowledge.

Jesus said Peter knew He was the Messiah because he had learned it from His Father in heaven, and not another human being (Matthew 16:17). He made it clear that Peter had "heart" knowledge of this fact. The teachers of religious law were experts in the scriptures. They had head knowledge and knew all the three-hundred-plus prophecies that foretold Jesus' coming, but they never recognized Him. Their head knowledge never made the trip eighteen inches downward into their hearts.

Heart knowledge is the key to knowing God. You don't just read or hear about Him as you would a good recipe. You taste Him. You savor Him. He satisfies your hunger. He nourishes your soul. Knowing Him keeps you strong so you can counter anything the enemy throws at you, including illness. The Spirit of God began communicating with the spirit He placed inside of you the moment you first believed. Whether written or spoken, you know His words are true, giving you real answers to real-world problems. Spirit to spirit. His heart to yours. Loving you, guiding you, protecting you. Because He is good. Taste and see.

## Prayer

*Jesus, I know in my head that You loved me so much You died for me. I know You have the power to heal and restore me. But I want more, Lord! I want to experience Your love, though it is too great for me to fully understand. Complete me, Lord, with all the fullness of life and power that only comes from You (Ephesians 3:19). Please show me all You want to be for me and show me especially in this season of healing.*

*Lord, give me a deep, insatiable hunger to know You. I want to know Your nature. I want to know Your heart. I want to know what You think, how You feel, and how You feel about me. I want to personally experience Your goodness! Help me to taste You and know firsthand that You are good.*

# Your Thirsty Soul

*O God, you are my God; I earnestly search for you.*
*My soul thirsts for you; my whole body longs for you in*
*this parched and weary land where there is no water.*
Psalm 63:1

His weary legs would no longer hold his weight. *Oh God! My God!* He dropped to his knees and began crawling along the rocky path through the twisted canyons of the Judean wilderness. The sun beat down on his back as dust filled his nostrils. His tongue stuck to the roof of his mouth. *Water. . . must have water.* But there was no sign of water. There was nothing ahead, nothing behind, no sign of life—just this dry, dusty, rocky path cutting through miles and miles of parched and weary desert land.

His entire body ached. Only God could rescue him. He leaned against a canyon wall seeking temporary reprieve from the sun. *Must rest. Must save my strength.* Once again, he surveyed his surroundings. There was nothing new. Nothing for miles except rocky wilderness. No life. Only dust and rocks. *But God, You alone are life. I know Your power. I have basked in Your glory. And I need You now! You are better than life itself!* He lifted his hands to the heavens, groping for Him, desperate to touch His face. *I praise You, God! Nothing else matters anymore. All my possessions, my reputation, the pleasure of this world, I count as garbage! You are enough. You alone satisfy my deepest longings. You alone quench my thirst.*

Time passed and darkness fell. He shivered in the cold desert air as he drifted in and out of sleep. *Oh God, fill my mind! Capture my thoughts and emotions! You are my helper and*

*I cling to You! I sing for joy!* He heard something moving in the shadows. It moved closer. He opened his eyes and strained to see. It kept moving closer until he felt it surrounding him from all sides. *Oh God, protect me under the shadow of Your wings! Hold me tight in Your strong right hand! Bring to ruin whatever is plotting to destroy me! Let my enemies be silenced; let them become food for the jackals! I praise You, Lord!* (Psalm 63).

Psalm 63 captures how King David yearned for God in times of his deepest distress. For years, he ran for his life from King Saul and his army who relentlessly sought to kill him. The Judean wilderness was his hiding place (1 Samuel 23–24), an area extending from just north of Jerusalem to the southern tip of the Dead Sea. Its Hebrew name, *Yeshimon*, describes it perfectly. It means "devastation." Like David's mouth thirsted for water in this dark and weary land, so his soul thirsted for God. His entire body ached with a yearning that only God could fill. Although he may not have understood what God was doing in the life of His future king, this wilderness time awakened his senses and gave him deeper spiritual understanding of God and His nature. His values and priorities changed. Intimacy with God took precedence over all the pleasures of the world. Nothing else mattered. God completely captured David's thoughts and emotions. He became his only source of satisfaction and fulfillment, the only One who could protect him and keep him safe. He was God and He was enough. The desert was his training ground for all that God had destined him to do.

You may be in the same desperate place as David. You know God's Word. You know He wishes you well. You know He is good. But you don't understand His ways. What you know of His nature and your current situation simply isn't lining up. Just like David, your soul cries out from the wilderness, desperate for His presence, desperate to understand His heart and mind. Dear one, He hears you. Let Him capture your thoughts and emotions. Let Him rearrange your priorities. Let Him satisfy your thirsty soul. He is enough. He alone can satisfy more than any other blessing that comes from His hand. In Him, you will never be thirsty again.

## Prayer

*Lord, my entire body aches for You in this parched and weary land. I know Your power. I have basked in Your glory. And I need You now! Lord, capture my thoughts and emotions! Protect me under the shadow of Your wings! Hold me tight in Your strong right hand! Bring to ruin this disease that is plotting to destroy me! Let my enemies be silenced. I praise You, Lord! You are my helper and I cling to You!*

*Lord, You are the only One who can save my life. You are life itself. No, You are better than life itself! I lift my hands to the heavens, Lord. I am desperate to touch Your face. I praise You, Lord! Nothing else matters. I count everything else as garbage! You are my everything, my all in all. You are enough. You alone satisfy my deepest longings. Lord, I want You even more than I want to be healed. You quench my thirsty soul.*

## Jehovah-Rapha: Mary's Story

She stared at the phone. The call would come soon. Surely, this must be a bad dream. No, a nightmare. A couple of weeks ago during a routine annual exam, her doctor found a lump on her left breast. Even though her recent mammogram was negative, the doctor remained suspicious. She followed her instincts and ordered an ultrasound "just to be sure." The ultrasound led to a biopsy and more waiting. Through all the waiting, she spent hours reading books and researching breast cancer symptoms on the Internet, looking for evidence to prove her doctor wrong. Or maybe gaining knowledge was her way of mastering a situation that was proving itself beyond her control. The phone finally rang, and everyone's suspicions were confirmed. "You have cancer," said the voice on the other end of the line.

It was surreal. She had no family history of cancer, only healthy parents and grandparents who lived long and full lives. Besides, cancer happened to other people. *Not to me*. Over the next few days, she walked around in a daze from phone call to phone call, appointment to appointment, and one test after another. She sifted through a mountain of information trying to make sense of her treatment options. She felt like she was drinking water from a fire hose. Finally the cloud began to lift, and things started to make sense. The tumor appeared very small, likely early stage. She would have a lumpectomy followed by a few weeks of radiation, and then she could put this all behind her and get on with her life.

After scheduling the surgery, she remembered the

prayer chapel in her church where people would go for prayer during services. She always thought prayer was something pastors did from the front of the church or something you did silently and privately before God. Every Sunday, she would watch people go in the chapel and always thought they must be really desperate. And then it dawned on her; she was really desperate. Impulsively, she took her family into the chapel and asked the prayer ministers to pray for her before the surgery. She was not prepared for what happened. They circled around her, and for the first time in her life, she *experienced* God. When they touched her, He touched her. When they anointed her head with oil, He anointed her head with oil. When they wiped away her tears, He wiped away her tears. She never had felt so close to the heart and mind of Christ. She never had felt so loved. They prayed for complete and total healing and restoration. And she believed.

She went into surgery filled with confidence. She felt God's presence with her, and she felt every prayer. But things didn't turn out the way everyone expected. It wasn't one lump; it was two. The cancer wasn't in the early stages. It had already spread to her lymph nodes. It wouldn't mean just a few weeks of radiation. It would mean several months of chemotherapy. It would mean side effects, like fatigue, nausea, numb hands and feet, and general joint and body aches. And it would mean baldness. Months and months of baldness.

She was suddenly thrust from a world of wellness into a world of the sick. She desperately wanted to live a "normal life"—to continue to work, take care of her family, and live as she had lived before. That would be difficult with so much of the day spent in hospital waiting rooms, labs, and chemo chairs. And it would be difficult without hair, eyebrows, and eyelashes. In the midst of this life-threatening crisis, losing her hair was surprisingly traumatic. She could receive treatment and keep her diagnosis private. But a bald head would announce her cancer to the world.

In an effort to maintain control, she bought a wig and had her long hair cut to match. When her hair began falling out seventeen days after the first treatment, her husband shaved it off. Then he said, "Wow, you have a beautifully shaped head. Let's go out for dinner." And they did. She was so grateful for a family that didn't treat her like a "sick person." And she avoided those who pitied her and acted as if she were dying.

As the months passed, something profound happened to her in this "dark bald place." God continued what He started in the prayer chapel. This confident wife, mom, and businesswoman who had always been in control, had lost control. She reached the end of herself and all her human abilities. All her degrees, accomplishments, experience, and intelligence would not be able to save her. Only God could save her. Naked and bald, she dropped to her knees and cried out to Him. She came face-to-face with her own brokenness, her mortality, her uncertain future, and her desperate need for a Savior. Everything she knew *about* God after a lifetime of going to church dropped eighteen inches from her head into her heart. She came to *know* God. All His promises and His love for her became real and personal. Jesus became more than Someone she thought about on Sunday mornings at church. He became Lord of her life.

On the last day of treatment, she realized the doctors could not give her the words she longed to hear. *You are healed.* It wasn't like pneumonia where she could take a prescribed course of antibiotics and be done with it. Doctors didn't know her prognosis. They could only give her statistics and chances of recurrences and monitor her vigilantly in the months and years ahead until her tests convinced them she was healed. At that point, she realized it was by His grace that she woke up every day before cancer, and it would be by His grace that she woke up every day after. She could live in fear from checkup to checkup, or she could live by faith in His perfect love. She chose faith. She chose God. Yes, she wanted His blessing. She wanted a long and full life. But she wanted Him more. He could take her home tomorrow, and He was all she needed. He was enough.

Fifteen years have passed, and she is healed and whole. She has devoted her life to ministering to others walking through a dark valley, to caring for the sick and hurting. She points them all to Jehovah-Rapha, the God who heals. Because whatever happens, He is enough.

# Dare to Believe

*The official pleaded, "Lord, please come now before my little boy dies."*
*Then Jesus told him, "Go back home. Your son will live!"*
*And the man believed what Jesus said and started home.*

JOHN 4:49–50

He was an important government official who worked for Herod Antipas. He had heard about this Healer named Jesus—the Jewish Messiah, some said. Many Galileans had been in Jerusalem at the Passover celebration and witnessed the miracles He performed there. People were excited to know He was traveling back from Judea to Galilee. After Jesus spent a couple of days in a Samaritan village preaching and sharing His message of the Kingdom, He stopped at Cana where He already had quite a reputation. It was here in Cana that He saved a wedding feast from disaster (and the host from embarrassment) by turning 180 gallons of water into wine!

And it was here, in Cana, that the government official hoped to find Jesus now. He was desperate. His little boy was very sick with a high fever and the doctors said there was nothing more they could do. His precious little boy was dying, and he, a reputable nobleman, could do absolutely nothing to save him. But Jesus could. It was barely dawn when he left home to walk over twenty miles through the countryside, barely stopping for rest, in hopes of convincing Jesus to come back to Capernaum with him. If He would just come with him, his son wouldn't die.

He arrived at the city gate and immediately began asking people where to find Jesus. A man of his stature had no problem getting people to cooperate, and quickly. A few townspeople led him to the place where Jesus was staying, and the homeowner immediately let him inside. A man on a mission, he went right up to Jesus and pleaded, "Lord, my son is about to die. Please come with me back to Capernaum and heal him. Please, Lord!" he begged. Knowing his noble stature, Jesus looked at him intently and asked, "Will you never believe in me unless you see miraculous signs and wonders?" But he ignored the Lord's question and continued to plead, "Lord, please come now before my little boy dies." Calmly and matter-of-factly, Jesus said, "Go back home. Your son will live!" At that moment, he believed what Jesus said was true. Without another word of pleading or coaxing, he turned around and walked out the door.

He rested well that evening and began the twenty-mile trek back to Capernaum at sunrise. While he was on his way, he spotted some men shouting and running toward him from a distance. When he got closer, he recognized some of his servants. "Master!" they shouted. "Your son is alive and well!" Relief and joy rushed through his body and tears flooded his eyes. *Thank You, Lord. Thank You.* Running toward them, he asked, "When did he start to get better?" They replied, "Yesterday afternoon at one o'clock his fever suddenly disappeared!" The official realized that was the very time Jesus had spoken the words, "Your son will live." He couldn't wait to get back home and embrace his little boy. He couldn't wait to tell his wife and relatives what had happened. And he couldn't wait to publicly praise Jesus and give Him all the glory. He did just that, and his entire household believed (John 4:43–54).

When this man humbled himself and called Jesus "Lord," he was addressing Him as someone who had authority over him, even though as a government official he had worldly authority over Jesus. He believed that Jesus was the Healer, and he proved it by walking twenty miles to plead for his son's life. Then he acted on his belief by walking twenty miles back home, taking Jesus at His word. Jesus was not impressed by the official's title. He was impressed by his faith. The official's faith resulted not only in the physical healing of his son, but in the spiritual healing of his entire household. You, too, can move the heart of God by acting on your faith. Don't just believe He can. Act as if He already did. Dare to believe.

## Prayer

*Lord, so often when I pray or others pray for me, I wait to see if You answer before I dare to believe. Please forgive my unbelief! I know nothing is impossible for You, but I want more! After I pray for healing, help me to take the next step of faith. Help me to act and think like a person who is completely whole! Help me to believe You and act on my belief.*

*Lord, I am so grateful that Your healing power is not limited by time or distance. Thank You for all those who keep me lifted up in prayer. Whether they pray from twenty miles away or right next to me, I know their faith moves Your heart. I dare to believe. May others believe when they see Your power at work in me. All for Your glory.*

# Go and Tell

*The man who had been freed from the demons begged to go with him. But Jesus sent him home, saying, "No, go back to your family, and tell them everything God has done for you." So he went all through the town proclaiming the great things Jesus had done for him.*
LUKE 8:38–39

He spotted Him climbing out of the boat. What was *He* doing in Gerasenes? What could He want? This could only mean trouble. He looked down at his naked, wretched body. For a long time he had been homeless and living among the burial caves outside of town. The people had given up on trying to restrain him. He always snapped the chains from his wrists and smashed the shackles. He smirked inside. He was stronger than all of them. Day and night he wandered among the burial caves and in the hills, howling and cutting himself with sharp stones. The townspeople could do nothing about it. They were too afraid of him. This was his territory and he controlled it. Now Jesus was here to ruin it all.

Shrieking at the top of his lungs, he ran down to meet Jesus and fell down in front of him. Then he screamed, "Why are you interfering with me, Jesus, Son of the Most High God? Please, I beg you, don't torture me!" Jesus had already spoken to the evil spirits that controlled him and commanded them to come out. "What is your name?" He demanded. The spirits replied, "My name is Legion, because there are many of us inside this man." The demons begged Him again and again not to send them to some distant place. There happened to be a large herd of pigs feeding on the hillside nearby, so the evil spirits pleaded, "Send us into those

**JEHOVAH-RAPHA:** *the God who heals* — **137**

pigs. Let us enter them!" Jesus gave them permission, and they came out of the man and entered the pigs. The entire herd of about two thousand plunged down the steep hillside into the lake and drowned in the water. Instantly, the man felt a dark, heavy burden lift off him. He was flooded with light and became aware of his surroundings and his nakedness. His mind was crystal clear. He looked up into the most beautiful, gentle eyes he had ever seen. He looked into the very face of love.

When the herdsmen saw it, they fled to the nearby town and the surrounding countryside, spreading the news. People rushed out to see what had happened, and a crowd gathered around Jesus. They were astounded to see the man sitting at Jesus' feet, fully clothed and perfectly sane. Terrified, they began pleading with Jesus to go away and leave them alone. As Jesus was getting into the boat, the healed man begged to go with Him. But Jesus said, "No, go back to your family, and tell them everything God has done for you." So he went all through the town proclaiming the great things Jesus had done for him (Mark 5:1–20; Luke 8:26–39).

Demons are still active today, and their goal is the same: to steal, kill, and destroy (John 10:10). They can distort and destroy your relationship with God by planting lies about Him and how He feels about you. They can cause mental and physical illness, block your blessing, and steal your destiny. This doesn't mean you must cower in fear, imagining a demon behind every corner. Demons are powerless against Jesus. This legion of evil spirits immediately recognized Him and knew His authority over them. In the same way, they are powerless against those who carry His presence. If you resist evil spirits in the name of Jesus and refuse to partner with their lies, they have no choice but to flee (James 4:7).

Sometimes people unknowingly allow evil spirits access to their lives by dabbling in occult activities like palm reading, tarot cards, and false religions. God clearly warns against these activities and calls them detestable (Deuteronomy 18:10–12). If we confess and renounce all past involvement, Jesus will cleanse and heal us (1 John 1:9).

Jesus healed this tormented man, and he became the first evangelist in this pagan Gerasene region. Don't be surprised if He also asks you to go and tell your family and friends the great things God has done for you!

## Prayer

*Lord, please reveal any lies I have believed about You and how You feel about me, and replace those lies with Your truth. Please show me any ways I may have sought wisdom or guidance from any spirits other than Yours. I renounce all ties with any activities that Your Word forbids, and if there is anything spiritual that is blocking my healing, I command it to leave in the name of Jesus! I receive Your forgiveness and cleansing, Lord!*

*Lord, thank You that by Your power and authority, my body, soul, and spirit are healed and set free. I shout from the rooftops the great things You have done for me!*

# Seek Him First

*"But seek first his kingdom and his righteousness,*
*and all these things will be given to you as well."*
MATTHEW 6:33 NIV

She was devastated. She had been battling for five long years. It might as well have been fifty. She couldn't remember what normal felt like. One treatment after another and all had failed. With each new drug, her hope would rise, only to crash into deep despair when the treatment disappointed. She had great hope for this one, a new clinical trial. After each treatment with this new experimental drug, they would test its effectiveness at killing the cancer cells that were devouring her lungs. The first test showed favorable results. The tumor had reduced by 11 percent. Tests after the second treatment showed 17 percent reduction. All looked good. *Could it be? Could this be the answer to my prayers?* She was more hopeful than she had felt in years. And then the phone rang. The doctor had the results after her third treatment. There was no reduction this time. Instead, the cancer was growing. He was sorry, but she no longer qualified for the study. They booted her out, and she had nowhere else to turn. There were no more treatments and no more studies. Nothing.

The pastor who ministered to her listened attentively to her story. "Where were you putting your trust?" she asked gently. Stunned, she thought for a minute and said, "Well, the new drug, I suppose. I thought this was God's answer to my prayers." The pastor continued, "And who created the doctors and the drugs?" She answered, "Well, God, of course." The pastor nodded and asked, "Then shouldn't you be placing your trust in God, the Creator, instead of the creation itself?" She leaned in. "He is the Lord of this study. He created it. Do you think He is upset because this drug didn't work?"

So often in our healing journey we find ourselves in this place. In our fear and desperation, we have allowed our trust in God the Creator to subtly shift to His creation. We put our trust in the new doctor and the latest treatments because these are tangible things we can touch and see. We forget who rules and reigns over it all. We must remember that doctors are human beings created by God and limited by human knowledge and wisdom. Their drugs and treatments are restricted by their capacity to work physiologically on the human body. God's power is boundless. Jesus offers something no human solution can offer.

Scripture promises that anyone who belongs to Christ has become a new person. The old life is gone, and a new life has begun (2 Corinthians 5:17)! But we can't be a new person until the old self completely dies. The only way for the old self to die is for us to place all our trust in God. The medical realm is all part of His blessing to us. He created it and He governs it. Can He withdraw His blessing (in this case, a study that didn't work) without our trust in Him being affected? We must reach a place in our healing journey where our faith in God and our trust in His promises *displace* our fear and unbelief—a place of simple trust where we no longer want only God's blessing, but we long for the Creator Himself.

Abundant medical research confirms better outcomes with faith and prayer. When the treatment works, praise Him! If it doesn't, praise Him and trust He has a better idea. Because nothing is impossible for Him (Matthew 19:26). "No thing" leaves Him upset or hopeless. He made it all. Whether the doctor cures you or you are healed supernaturally without a medical explanation, God gets the credit and the glory. Seek Him first, not the blessings that come from Him. Seek Him above all else, and He will give you everything you need.

## Prayer

*Father, forgive me for allowing my trust to shift from You to the blessings that come directly from Your hands. Thank You that Your power is unlimited, that You offer what no human solution can offer. I am a new creation in You, Lord. Let my old self completely die! Help my faith to displace all my fears and all my unbelief.*

*Lord, in You "no thing" is impossible. "No thing" is too hard for You. Why would I put my trust in an imperfect world with imperfect people and human limitations when I can put all my trust in a perfect God who is limitless? I seek You, Lord. I seek You first. Thank You for Your promise to give me everything I need.*

# Forever

*For the L*ORD *is good. His unfailing love continues forever,*
*and his faithfulness continues to each generation.*
PSALM 100:5

A recent Twitter conversation went something like this:

Well-Known Pastor @WellKnownPastor:
*"God wants you to have an amazing life."*

Godless @Godless:
*@WellKnownPastor: "Then He should stop riddling*
*people with cancer and other crippling diseases."*

Most likely, Godless or someone she loves has suffered from a life-threatening or crippling disease, and she has concluded that God is to blame. Instead of being a good God who wants her and others to have an amazing life, He is a mean, cruel, and vindictive God who makes people sick. This mindset can often originate from believing lies about God and His nature, or simply believing that we are not worthy of His love.

While a serious diagnosis can tempt even the strongest believer to doubt the nature of God, He did not make you sick and it is not His will that you should suffer! On the contrary, Satan is the thief whose purpose is to steal, kill, and destroy (John 10:10). Regardless of your beliefs about Satan, no one can deny there is evil in the world, and no one would deny that sickness is evil. It's important to put the blame where the blame belongs; if it steals, kills, and destroys, we can be certain it's not God. Satan is the culprit behind any sickness that threatens to destroy you. That's why Peter warns us to stay alert and strong in our faith (1 Peter 5:8), and Paul admonishes us to be strong in the Lord's power so we can stand firm against the strategies and tricks of the devil (Ephesians 6:11). Jesus warned us that one of Satan's tricks is to use every means possible to distract your attention and devotion from God and His Word (Mark 4:14–19).

If you believe your illness came from God, it might be difficult to ask Him for healing. Yes, God can certainly use your suffering for His glory and purposes (Romans 8:28), but that doesn't mean it originated with Him. It's difficult to trust God for something you believe is contrary to His plan for you, but His desire is to give you a life of abundance (John 10:10). When Jesus was on earth, He didn't inflict people with disease and calamity. He healed and delivered them (Acts 10:36–38). Jesus said if you have seen Him, you have seen His Father (John 14:9). If you want to know how God feels about you, just study the life of His Son. He overflowed with love and compassion for the sick and hurting (Matthew 14:14). Every person who came to Him left healed and free.

God's nature is to love because God is love (1 John 4:8). He created you out of love, and you are perfectly and wonderfully made, a precious masterpiece in His eyes (Psalm 139:14; Ephesians 2:10). His love for you knows no boundaries (Hosea 14:4), and His love is everlasting (Jeremiah 31:3). He loved you so much that He personally carried your sins and sickness in His own body on the cross (Isaiah 53:5). He showed you real love, a love through His Son that never ends (1 John 4:9–10).

How do you respond to a love like this when troubles come? You can turn from God in anger and unbelief. You can blame Him when the enemy comes to steal, kill, and destroy. You can turn away from the only One who can help you, the

One who has already conquered sin, crippling diseases, and everything the enemy throws at you. Or you can run into His arms for strength, comfort, and healing. Because He is *always* faithful. He is *always* good. And His love is forever.

## Prayer

*Lord, forgive me if I've believed lies about Your nature, that You are capable of being mean and cruel and the source of my afflictions. I'm so sorry for my doubt and unbelief and for turning my back on You in times of trouble! Help me to stand strong in Your power and firm in my faith against the distractions of the enemy. You died and rose again so I can be free of sin and crippling diseases and so I can resist all the enemy's strategies and tricks.*

*Thank You for the gift of abundant life! I run into Your arms, Lord. I choose You! I receive Your love and compassion! I come to You for complete healing and restoration. I want all You died for, Jesus. I want You to receive the full reward for Your suffering! Thank You for choosing me first, for loving me with a real love that stands the test of time, a perfect love that never ends and never fails. Regardless of my circumstances, You are good. You are always good. Your love continues forever!*

# No Condemnation

*So now there is no condemnation*
*for those who belong to Christ Jesus.*
Romans 8:1

She came into the prayer chapel reluctantly, her friend at her side and her head lowered, unable to make eye contact with the prayer minister who greeted them. They found a comfortable place to sit, and the prayer minister asked how she could help. Her friend did all the talking. "This is my friend Vicki. We work together and she was just diagnosed with cancer. I've been inviting her to come to church with me and I'm so happy she agreed to come today. I told her we have people who will pray for her." Smiling, the prayer minister turned to Vicki and said, "It's good to meet you. I'm so sorry for your diagnosis. I'm sure this was devastating news for you. But you have come to the right place. We are honored to pray with you." Vicki shrugged. "It's okay. I figured something like this would happen sooner or later." Looking intently at the friend who brought her, she continued, "You can pray, but I probably brought this on myself. My mom and I stopped going to church years ago, about the time my dad left us. I tried praying, but nothing ever happened, so I stopped."

The prayer minister said softly, "Tell me more about your dad." "There's not much to tell, really," Vicki said. "He took me hunting once in a while. We played catch." She paused and reflected. "I always thought he wished I was a boy." Then she added wistfully, "We really didn't see him much after he left. He sent money. He and his new wife had kids of their own. I felt like an intruder the few times I went to stay with them, so I stopped going."

Vicki's past experiences with her earthly father had distorted her view of her heavenly Father—how she thought He saw her, and how she saw herself. Fathers meet our needs for identity, security, protection, and provision. We learn we are lovable and valuable based on how Dad treats us. If he is not around physically or emotionally, we can get confused about who we are and start believing that we are unworthy of love or that we are a great disappointment to him. If Dad isn't there when scary things happen, we can feel vulnerable. It becomes very difficult to connect with a heavenly Father who we think is distant, cold, mad at us, punishing us, or can't be trusted. Through ministry, Vicki was able to forgive her dad and allow the Holy Spirit to heal her wounds and replace the lies she had believed about herself and God with the truth that she *is* worthy of God's love and all His blessings and that He will *never* abandon her.

In the same way, God is not using sickness as a way of punishing you for not praying enough or not going to church enough, or because you are a great disappointment to Him or unworthy of His love. He is not using illness to teach you a lesson, to get even, or to get your attention. It is not in His character to treat you this way. He came to save the world, not to judge it (John 3:17). His compassion and love for you are unlimited, and nothing in all creation, no mistake you could ever make, no power in the sky above or in the earth below, can separate you from His love that is revealed in Christ (Romans 8:38–39). You are His child and He is a *perfect* Daddy. If you are struggling to accept this truth and you have children of your own, consider this question: Would you strike your own children with a devastating disease and abandon them as a punishment for their mistakes? No, not likely. If we as imperfect people know how to give good gifts to our children, then how much more will our Lord give good gifts to us (Matthew 7:9–11)? There is no condemnation in Him. None.

## Prayer

*Heavenly Father, please reveal any lies that I have believed about You. I choose to forgive my earthly father. I'm sorry for agreeing with the lie that You are anything like my earthly dad. By the authority of Jesus and in His name, I renounce the lie that You, Father God, would treat me the same way, that You are cold and distant, that You would abandon me, leave me unprotected, or withhold Your love from me.*

*Thank You for being the perfect Daddy. I receive the truth that You will never leave me or forsake me, that I am Your precious child, worthy of Your love, security, and protection, and You will provide for all my needs. I choose to bless my earthly father. I release him to You. Please give me an accurate picture of who You are and how You see me. I receive Your truth, Lord. Nothing can separate me from Your love. You delight in me! In You, I am healed and whole. In You, there is no condemnation.*

## Jehovah-Rapha: Diane's Story

Her eyes blazed. She was angry. Angry at her doctors. Angry at her family. Angry at herself. Angry at God. The ministry appointment had been scheduled for several weeks now, and she almost didn't come today. She didn't know why they made her leave the hospital. They had pumped her up with fluids and nutrition and made her eat. They sent a shrink in to talk to her, and they scheduled another time to meet. *Yeah, right.* She even met with a nutritionist who prescribed a daily diet to gain weight. The doctor wouldn't continue the chemo until she could eat, stay hydrated, and stop dropping weight. Instead, he gave her some IV meds to strengthen her bones. *Fine, they can blame* him *when I die.* Today, she drove herself to the appointment, even though she was weak and dizzy and could barely stand up on her own. Probably because she'd skipped breakfast. And maybe dinner the night before. She couldn't remember. It didn't matter.

Her children were of no help. Busy, always busy. Too busy for her. And *her mother*? All she could do was tell her all the ways she had screwed up her life. And harp on her to eat, of course. Well, she was an adult and didn't need anyone to tell her to eat. If she wanted to skip a meal now and then, that was her business. Never, how are you *doing*, Diane? Never a real interest in knowing the truth. While her mother was badgering her to eat, her sister was pestering her to have more *faith*. She needed to go to church. She needed *Jesus*. It was her sister who had insisted on this ministry appointment. She looked at the pastor and her associate with defiant eyes, wondering why in the world she had come. No one lives long with stage 4 breast cancer anyway, especially when their doctors won't even give them the treatment necessary to fight it.

They chatted. Small talk, mostly. The pastor prayed. Now it was time to get to work. To get personal. They talked about her family. They asked her about Father God, Jesus, and the Holy Spirit, how she viewed each part of the Trinity, and what He thought of her. She gave them some good descriptions, right out of her Sunday school memories, and they seemed to be satisfied. They guided her through some prayers as she forgave her parents and her siblings for a variety of offenses she had held against them throughout her lifetime. She felt a little better. She looked at her watch, hoping it would be over soon.

Then the floodgates opened. The pastor started talking about one of the doors that the enemy can enter to gain a foothold in our lives: the door of *hatred*. She closed her eyes and saw a red, fiery door, too hot to touch. On the other side was a beautiful, peaceful open meadow. Jesus was there and His arms were outstretched. But she couldn't get to Him. The door was aflame and she couldn't get through it. She couldn't get close. Her heart pounded in her chest. *Need to get out of here.* But she couldn't move.

The pastor's voice interrupted her thoughts. "What is God showing you?" she asked. She described the door, and the pastor guided her to pray. "Lord, who do I need to forgive?" she heard herself pray out loud as tears poured down her cheeks. Immediately, the Lord brought her ex-husband to the forefront of her mind. *Of course.*

She could never please him. She wasn't pretty enough or smart enough. Her body wasn't perfect enough. His trophy wife? Now *she* was perfect. Then He brought her adult children to mind, each one by name. They always took *his* side. She was too negative. She complained all the time. She often spent holidays alone, while they were with *his* family.

He brought up other things, too. Childhood wounds she had long forgotten. Times past when she had disappointed her mother; when her father didn't fight for her; when she failed to measure up to her sister, no matter how hard she tried—all situations where the wounds had turned to anger, and the anger turned to bitterness. It wasn't fair. Her whole life wasn't fair. Layers and layers of anger and bitterness had formed a tough exterior that simply deadened the pain.

One by one, she chose to forgive them for not being the husband, children, parents, and siblings she needed them to be. She repented for believing the lie that the Lord would treat her the same way, that He was unfair, and that she was unworthy of His forgiveness, His love, and His blessing. She asked forgiveness for holding on to hatred, bitterness, and offense. She renounced the lie that her anger, bitterness, and unforgiveness would somehow settle the score, and released every one of them into the Lord's hands. Finally, she forgave herself for failing as a daughter, wife, and mother. She was overwhelmed by the Lord's grace and overpowered by His love. A huge weight lifted off her tiny shoulders as the Holy Spirit washed over her, healing every wound and replacing every lie that held her hostage to bitterness with the truth and presence of Jesus. By the end of the session, she walked through the smoldering door of hatred and closed it behind her, right into His outstretched arms. Waves and waves of His love flowed through her as she wept.

Before she left, the ministry team laid hands on her and prayed for physical healing. She felt peace fall over her like never before. When she stood up to leave, she was amazed to discover all her strength had returned. Her head was clear and she was no longer dizzy. She felt good, better than she could remember in a long time. She even felt hungry. A few days later, she went in for a scan to assess how the cancer was progressing. The report stunned her doctor but confirmed what she already knew. The cancer was gone. The aggressive form of cancer that he said she "would never recover from" was completely gone. Praise Jehovah-Rapha, Healer of the body, soul, and spirit. He delivered her from the prison of bitterness, and He healed her body, too. He made her whole again.

# Be Opened!

*Looking up to heaven, he sighed and said, "Ephphatha,"*
*which means, "Be opened!" Instantly the man could hear perfectly,*
*and his tongue was freed so he could speak plainly!*

MARK 7:34–35

He was a sickly little boy who had suffered from many fevers. He vaguely remembered the soft sound of his mother's voice, his father's instructions when he helped with chores, the sounds of the animals, and the laughter of his friends playing in the streets. His parents began noticing how he misunderstood their directions or ignored them altogether. He grew listless and withdrew into his own little world. Now as an adult, he had learned to live with his deafness. He loved being around his friends, but it frustrated him not to fully participate in their conversations. He watched their lips and they made hand motions, communicating the best they could. He tried talking back, but it required patience to listen to him. His strange speech often sounded like garbled noise. He longed to know what they were thinking or feeling. Something was sorely missing in his relationships. Now, his friends wanted to change all that.

It shouldn't be too difficult for some determined Galileans traveling with a deaf man with a speech impediment to find the Healer. They had heard He'd left Tyre and gone up to Sidon, and now was taking a roundabout way back to the Sea of Galilee through Decapolis, the region of the Ten Towns. His friends had sketched it all out for him in the dirt as they set out on their mission. From what he could tell, it was there they hoped to find Him. They had crossed the Jordan south of the Sea of Galilee; he was trapped in his silent world while his friends visited with the people they met along the way. They were apparently successful, because he was certain it was Jesus they could see up ahead on the outskirts of a nearby town. He was surrounded by a crowd of people. His friends took off running, and he followed close at their heels. Pushing through the crowd, they approached Jesus, their hands and mouths moving all at once as they pointed to him.

Jesus studied him for a moment. The deaf man looked back into the kindest eyes he had ever seen. He barely had time to process that Jesus could actually *heal* him, when He put His arm around his shoulder and led him away from the crowd. When they were a good distance away, He stopped. Placing His hands on both shoulders, Jesus looked at him again. *Those eyes.* Then Jesus did the strangest thing. He put His fingers into his deaf ears! Then He spit on His fingers and touched his locked tongue. Jesus looked up, His chest lowered, and he felt His breath. Then He said something. It must have been something powerful, because instantly his ears popped, and the sounds he vaguely remembered from his youth rushed in. He could hear perfectly! Words of joy spilled out of his mouth, and they came out flawlessly. He could speak plainly. *Praise You, Jesus!*

He ran back to the crowd to tell his friends what Jesus had done, and they were completely amazed, shouting with joy along with him. Even though Jesus told them not to tell anyone, they couldn't help themselves, and said again and again, "Everything He does is wonderful. He even makes the deaf to hear and gives speech to those who cannot speak" (Mark 7:31–37).

Jesus sighed, showing empathy for this man and the disability that hindered his relationships with other people.

He grieved that he was missing out on the full life His Father desired for him. And He showed us again that we can't dictate the methods He will use to heal and restore. Sometimes He spoke; sometimes He touched. Here, He spat and touched the man's ears and tongue. In the same way, He may heal us instantly or heal over time; He may heal supernaturally or heal through the medical realm. He may heal our physical bodies by first healing our soul. We can rejoice that we will always be healed in heaven. And like Jesus, we can look up, knowing that all healing comes directly from our Father's hands.

By uttering *Ephphatha*, Aramaic for "be opened," Jesus intentionally referenced Isaiah's prophesy: "And when he comes, he will open the eyes of the blind and unplug the ears of the deaf. The lame will leap like a deer, and those who cannot speak will sing for joy!" (Isaiah 35:5–6). Yes, indeed, your long-awaited Messiah has come. May your heart be opened to receive!

## Prayer

*Lord, like the crowd who watched Your miracles, I stand amazed. Everything You do is wonderful! You are so good! I know You want the best for me, and I know You identify with my suffering. You suffer with me because You suffered for me. You are no stranger to my pain. You are the Messiah, the Anointed One, my Savior.*

*Thank You that You always heal. I know Your methods are of Your own choosing. Have mercy on me, Lord. Let nothing stand in the way of my walking in the fullness of life. Let nothing block my healing. Unplug my ears so I can hear. Open my heart so I can receive. My mouth sings for joy! Let me hear You cry, "Ephphatha!"*

# Out of the Pit

*Jesus asked the Pharisees and experts in religious law, "Is it permitted in the law to heal people on the Sabbath day, or not?" When they refused to answer, Jesus touched the sick man and healed him and sent him away.*
LUKE 14:3–4

He had no idea why they had invited him. It's not every day someone gets a personal invitation to the home of the lead Pharisee for Sabbath dinner. He was a good, hardworking man, well liked in the community, but certainly not one of them. His distinguished host met him at the door and led him to his seat. He tried to engage the religious leader in some polite conversation, but the host seemed disinterested. *Why invite me?* He had dressed carefully, trying to cover the swelling in his arms and legs as best he could. Maybe they wouldn't notice. He coughed and cleared his throat, feeling the congestion in his lungs. The walk here had left him short of breath. He was lost in his thoughts when another guest arrived. It was Jesus. Jesus of Nazareth. Now he was really confused. *Why would they invite me to a gathering of religious leaders?*

As they waited for dinner, he noticed everyone was watching Jesus closely, murmuring to one another in hushed tones. Jesus sat in silence, His eyes panning the room. He stopped when the sick man met His stare. After studying him for a few seconds, Jesus looked up and asked the religious leaders, "Is it permitted in the law to heal people on the Sabbath day, or not?" Silence. They refused to answer. He watched as Jesus moved toward him. Saying nothing, He touched him. A strange power surged through his body, and

Jesus leaned in and told him to go. Without saying a word, he headed for the door, with all swelling and symptoms gone, and not quite sure what had just happened or why. On his way out, he heard Jesus say, "Which of you doesn't work on the Sabbath? If your son or your cow falls into a pit, don't you rush to get him out?" Again, silence. Bounding for home, he realized he never had his dinner. Instead, Jesus healed him. And he hadn't even asked. Surprised and overwhelmed, he marveled at the grace of God. Jesus had pulled him out of the pit (Luke 14:1–6).

The man was healed, but Jesus was in trouble again. The long list of "dos and don'ts" the religious leaders added to God's law over the centuries had once again taken priority over the needs of people. The law required them to rest on the Sabbath (Exodus 20:8), and since healing was "work," they accused Jesus of defying the law. In fact, He healed on the Sabbath at least seven times. In addition to this man with edema, He healed a man of a demon (Mark 1:21–28), Peter's mother-in-law of fever (Mark 1:29–31), a lame man by the pool (John 5:1–18), a man with a deformed hand (Mark 3:1–6), a crippled woman (Luke 13:10–17), and a man born blind (John 9:1–16). Through healings and several other clashes with the Pharisees and religious leaders, He continued to challenge their man-made rules, structures, and traditions by demonstrating the true purpose of the law—to honor God by helping people in need. The Sabbath was created *for* people, not the other way around (Mark 2:27).

If the Pharisees invited this man to trap Jesus into breaking the law, it was no surprise to Jesus. He used the illustration of a child or a cow falling into a pit to challenge their callous, legalistic, hypocritical thinking. Likewise, this man's life was in a dangerous pit. His swelling and water retention were signs that he quite possibly suffered from congestive heart failure, a life-threatening condition caused by heart disease. Jesus lifted him out of the pit of sickness and set his feet on solid ground (Psalm 40:2). Jesus gave him exactly what he needed, and the man didn't even ask. He can do the same for you. He knows your every need (Matthew 6:7–8). Before you call out, He answers (Isaiah 65:24). Let Him pull you out of the pit.

## Prayer

*Jesus, thank You that Your mercy and compassion overrule the laws and rules of man. Thank You that You extend Your grace to me when I least expect it and that You know the depth of my need before I even cry out Your name! Thank You for setting the answers to my prayers in motion before I even think to pray.*

*Lord, forgive me when I doubt Your ways. I don't always understand what's going on around me. I'm not certain what will happen tomorrow or how my healing fits into Your plans and purposes. But I know I can be certain of You. I know You love me, and I know You are good. Lord, I have fallen into a pit of sickness and despair. But I trust You. Please have mercy. Pull me out of the pit!*

# Small as a Mustard Seed

*The apostles said to the Lord, "Show us how to increase our faith."*
*The Lord answered, "If you had faith even as small as a mustard seed,*
*you could say to this mulberry tree, 'May you be uprooted and*
*thrown into the sea,' and it would obey you!"*

LUKE 17:5–6

Susan sat in the circle with others in the cancer prayer and support group, waiting for her turn to "check in." The pastor facilitating the group had given instructions. After introducing themselves, they should give a brief update and any praises, prayer requests, or concerns they would like to share. It was her first night and she was nervous. Listening to the stories around the circle, she was even more unsettled. She didn't belong here. Some of the "regulars" praised God for answering their prayers for healing. Others shared their latest victories or setbacks. In spite of their dire circumstances, they all seemed to have hope. *Don't they understand this is cancer we're dealing with?* Her brother-in-law was right. She needed more faith. A lot more. Without it, *her* story wouldn't end well. And he should know. He was a leader in his church. The sound of her name pulled her out of her thoughts. It was her turn. She cleared her throat. "My name is Susan. I have uterine cancer." She paused. Tears welled up and her thoughts spilled out. "And I'm afraid I don't have enough faith to be healed."

Faith is expecting the God of the Bible to do what He says He will. It is the confident assurance that what we hope for will actually happen and assurance of the evidence of things we cannot yet see (Hebrews 11:1). Some believers, like

Susan, fear they don't have enough faith or have been told they lack faith by well-meaning Christians. If they just had more, they would receive their healing. If this has been your experience, the church owes you an apology.

It's true that Jesus healed everyone who came to Him, and He often told people their faith had made them well. Unfortunately, our human mind can turn this truth into something like this: *if* people are healed because of their faith, *then* those who aren't healed don't have enough. But it's not that simple. We can't put God in a box and apply our human logic to supernatural things. Who can possibly explain these real-life examples?

- Before becoming a pastor, a woman with no faith at all is supernaturally healed of stage 4 cancer.
- A pastor who doesn't believe in modern-day miracles prays for someone who is immediately healed.
- A young man well known for his strong faith who is covered in prayer by an army of prayer warriors loses his battle to cancer.
- Two women of faith receive exactly the same life-threatening diagnosis, but only one is healed and survives.

It's not up to us to sort all this out, nor should we. We will always encounter mysteries in our walk with Jesus. But our faith in Him must never be contingent on our experiences or our ability to figure Him out. The very foundation of Christianity is that our salvation is by grace through *faith alone* in what Christ has done, so none can boast (Ephesians 2:8–9).

How much faith is enough? The apostles wanted to know, too. Jesus said a mustard seed of faith was enough for a tree to be uprooted and thrown into the sea at their command. If you have ever held a mustard seed, you know it is very, very small. The amount of faith you have is not as important as the type of faith and the posture of your heart. Just showing up at the prayer meeting was an act of faith for Susan. The Lord can do big things with a humble and obedient heart and a small amount of genuine faith.

## Prayer

*Lord, in Your name, I break off any words spoken over me that I don't have enough faith to be healed. I'm sorry for believing the lie that You will withhold healing and blessing from me if I lack faith. Forgive me if I have made my understanding of You and Your ways a requirement for believing in Your promises. Thank You that there is no condemnation in You (Romans 8:1). Thank You for Your grace that covers me when I struggle with doubt.*

*Help me reach a place in my relationship with You where my trust in You and Your promises completely displaces all my doubts and fears. I give You my heart, Lord. Please give me a genuine faith and the willingness to trust and obey. My faith may be small as a mustard seed, but in You and by Your power, I can toss my burdens into the sea!*

# Prayer of Faith

*Are any of you sick? You should call for the elders of the church to come and pray over you, anointing you with oil in the name of the Lord. Such a prayer offered in faith will heal the sick, and the Lord will make you well. And if you have committed any sins, you will be forgiven.*

JAMES 5:14–15

She stood in the doorway of the dimly lit chapel with her husband. She hoped they had found the right place. Her friend had given clear instructions, and they had traveled over a hundred miles to get here. They hesitated, not knowing what to do, and quickly breathed a sigh of relief at the smiling face coming toward them. "Good morning!" the man greeted them warmly. "Have you come for prayer?" "Oh, yes!" she exclaimed. "We are Bill and Sandy. We came from a small town south of here." As the prayer minister led them to some seats in the corner, Sandy was quick to explain, "My friend's daughter comes to this church, and we heard the ministers here will pray over people and anoint them when they are sick." They both sat down facing the prayer minister and she continued, "I have lung cancer and I'm starting treatment soon." Bill jumped in. "We wanted to bring all this to the Lord and receive prayer from the church elders."

In the Bible, our manual for living, God gives clear instructions for what to do if we get physically sick. Bill and Sandy were being obedient to God's instructions. They went to the church and asked a ministry leader to pray *over* Sandy for healing. Church leaders should always be responsive to the needs of its members and be available to come alongside people like Bill and Sandy and pray for them. The prayer of faith is part of the healing process because God gives the people of His church the privilege of co-laboring with Him in His redemptive work (1 Corinthians 3:9; 2 Corinthians 5:18–20).

Sadly, too many people turn to fervent prayer as a last resort after they have exhausted all other options to get well. Like Bill and Sandy, we should invite Jesus into the middle of our battle from the beginning. He can provide comfort and encouragement as well as wisdom and revelation to heal or guide the healing process. Our God is a gentleman, and He often waits for us to ask before He intervenes. He will not barge in where He isn't invited. He also won't tolerate our seeking Him for healing along with other gods and new-age remedies because "every little bit helps" and "it can't hurt." Indeed, it *can* hurt. He alone is God, and all healing comes from Him. He will not share our affections with any other spirit but His (Exodus 20:5).

A team of prayer ministers gathered around Sandy, prayed for healing, and anointed her with oil. In the Bible, oil had both medical and spiritual properties. The Good Samaritan used oil as a salve to soothe the wounds of the Jewish man who was beaten by bandits (Luke 10:34). God's prophets used oil to anoint kings, setting them apart for God's service (1 Samuel 16:13). In a similar way, God can use both the medical and spiritual realms to heal. Going to the doctor and seeking God for healing through prayer are not mutually exclusive activities. Both the faith and medical communities work together with God to care for a whole person made of body, soul, and spirit (1 Thessalonians 5:23).

God will always give us wisdom to make the best healthcare decisions if we ask Him in faith (James 1:5–8). Sometimes, a sick person might believe that God wants to heal supernaturally and refuse some or all medical treatments. It is critical to make sure such decisions are not driven by ungodly motives such as fear of the treatment itself, denial, or the desire to receive a "higher form" of healing. Healing through the medical realm is not somehow inferior to a miraculous healing. One type does not require more faith than another. God is the Healer, regardless. Whether healing comes with or without medical intervention, we praise God for His grace and goodness and give Him the glory. His will is to heal, and the prayer of faith moves His heart.

## Prayer

*Lord, I come to You in faith. I invite You into the very center of my illness. Come, Holy Spirit, come. I need Your wisdom and revelation. Please show me a clear path to wellness, spiritually and medically. Help me not to doubt or waver. Forgive me for sharing my worship or seeking healing from any other spirit but Yours, Lord. Thank You for giving me the best of science and the best of Jesus.*

*Lord, please lead me to a church where the leaders will pray over me and anoint me with oil according to Your Word. I believe their prayer offered in faith will heal me, and You will make me well. Thank You for your grace and goodness. I give You the glory.*

# Go. . .Till He Says No

*"My sheep listen to my voice;*
*I know them, and they follow me."*
JOHN 10:27

"I don't know what to do. There are just too many options, and no one agrees. The more information I get, the more confused I become. I'm so overwhelmed," Calvin lamented to his pastor. He had several consults with numerous doctors from many reputable clinics. One wanted to do surgery immediately. Another wanted to watch and wait. Still another wanted to try a new drug therapy that was effective but had many untoward side effects. A friend whose wife was a nurse told him about another doctor, and he was considering seeking another medical opinion. Still another friend had a friend with the same condition, and raved about the new drug therapy. "Have you asked God what He thinks?" asked the pastor. Calvin looked surprised. "Well, no. He'll talk to me? He'll answer a specific question like that?"

Yes, Calvin. He will. Jesus said that His followers would be able to hear His voice, and He planted the Holy Spirit inside us as the perfect transmitter (John 16:13). When we need answers, we read His Word, pray, wait, and trust. The Bible is the inspired Word of God and our standard for testing everything else that claims to be true. Through it, He brings clarity to our thinking and equips us to do what is right (2 Timothy 3:16–17). When you read the scriptures, the Holy Spirit within you brings the words to life and makes the Word personal to your specific needs and prayers. The Spirit can speak through verses you may have read countless times in the past, bringing fresh revelation to a current dilemma.

When Elijah sought God's voice, God told him that His voice would not be found in the mighty windstorm, the earthquake, or the fire, but in the sound of a gentle whisper (1 Kings 19:11–12). He can speak to you through that same gentle whisper, but you need to get into position to hear by removing your own distractions. You might take a quiet walk in nature, or recline in a chair and rest in the silence. Or some soft intimate worship music might help you quiet your soul and prepare you to draw close to God. Focus your mind on Jesus and invite the Holy Spirit to come. Give the Spirit permission to reveal Himself according to His will. Don't try to analyze things or push too hard for answers. Just rest in faith and trust that God is working within you. When you make it a habit to wait before Him in rest, the Holy Spirit speaks to your own spirit, your spirit speaks His message to your mind, and your mind eventually knows what to do.

There are other ways to hear God's voice. Some people are gifted in prophecy (Romans 12:6; Ephesians 4:11). If someone shares a word from God that you believe directly relates to your situation, be sure to test that word against scripture (1 Thessalonians 5:20–21). The purpose of prophecy is to edify, encourage, and bring comfort (1 Corinthians 14:3). Does the word of prophecy align with the Bible, or does it contradict the Word of God and His character? God can also speak in dreams and visions (Genesis 28:11–19; 37:5–11; Acts 2:17). Always test to make sure that any spirit that speaks to you through a prophetic word, dream, or vision is truly from God (1 John 4:1–2).

Calvin listened to the voice of man, *many* voices, and the result was confusion. Seeking godly counsel is not wrong (Psalm 37:30–31; Proverbs 27:9). But you should always go to God first. When God leads you to seek the counsel of man, make sure the person is filled with goodness and able to speak truth (Romans 15:14). They should be knowledgeable about the Bible and able to discern good from evil (Hebrews 5:13–14). Never seek the counsel of the ungodly (Psalm 1:1–3) and never view the counsel of man as the final authority. In all circumstances, seek God's truth and confirmation through His Word and prayer.

When a decision is required, act with the best revelation you have. Sometimes, you may have to move forward with no clear confirmation from God and trust that doors will close if you're headed in the wrong direction. Often, there will be a persistent uneasiness or "check" in your spirit if you are moving outside of God's plan. If He doesn't stop you, don't doubt yourself. Go. . .till He says no.

## Prayer

*Lord, I am overwhelmed by all the options and opinions of man. But I know You are not a God of confusion. You are the Good Shepherd, and I am a sheep in Your fold. You promised I would hear Your voice. Today I bring all my thoughts captive to Your authority (2 Corinthians 10:5). As I seek Your heart, please order my thoughts and bring clarity to my situation.*

*Lord, lead me to scripture that will reveal Your truth. Help me linger in Your presence so I can hear Your still, small voice. You have given me a sound mind, not a spirit of fear (2 Timothy 1:7). I trust I have the mind of Christ (1 Corinthians 2:16). I move forward in faith and trust You will speak to me. I trust You to reveal Your truth and Your ways.*

## Jehovah-Rapha: Zach's Story

Jason and Lisa sat around the circle holding their beautiful baby boy in their arms. Lisa thought about the roller coaster of emotions she had been riding over the last seven months. She remembered the joy and elation she felt when she first looked into the face of her infant son Zachary and how he looked absolutely perfect. He had all ten fingers and all ten toes, his matted blond locks framing a chubby little face with bright blue eyes and a tipped-up nose. She watched in fascination as he moved through each stage of development. His first smile, the look on his face when he first rolled over by himself, his little personality emerging through his kicking, cooing, scooting, and giggling—it was perfection. She never imagined she would end up in a place like this. Jason found it in the church bulletin. It was a prayer group for people battling cancer. And she was here, with her perfect little boy. It was surreal. Tears welled up.

She told Jason she wouldn't talk; he would have to do all the talking. She just couldn't. She vaguely remembered someone greeting them warmly when they arrived. A pastor, she thought. Now she was asking Jason to introduce them to the rest of the group. Jason cleared his throat. Lisa just rocked Zach back and forth. "I am Jason. This is my wife, Lisa, and our son, Zachary," he began. "We came tonight because our son. . ." He struggled with the words. "Our baby boy has just been diagnosed"—his voice broke—"with a rare form of lung cancer." Lisa felt the tears she had been holding back stream down her cheeks. Someone handed her a box of tissues. A kind woman touched her shoulder. Zachary had been leaning against his mother's chest, but now his head bobbed up attentively, as if he somehow knew this was all about him.

Jason continued to tell their story. During a routine checkup, Zach's pediatrician noticed his breathing was very shallow. He ordered a chest X-ray that revealed a large dark mass on Zach's right lung. He was immediately admitted to the hospital. The doctor thought it was a type of cyst that can sometimes form in fetuses. In addition, Zach was suffering from a respiratory virus. It was devastating to watch their little boy disappear behind the doors of the surgical suite. But the surgery went well, and they breathed a huge sigh of relief. Zach spent a few more days in the hospital and then went home to fully recover from the surgery and the viral infection.

A couple of weeks later, they brought him back to the pediatrician for a routine follow-up visit. Routine, they thought, until the doctor delivered news that would change their lives forever. The cyst removed from Zach's chest was malignant. He had an extremely rare form of childhood lung cancer known as pleuropulmonary blastoma, so rare that only ten to twenty cases are diagnosed in the entire United States each year. There is only a handful of experts in the world who focus on this disease, and *two* of them practice in their city. "A reason for praise," someone in the group commented. "Absolutely," Jason agreed.

He took a breath and paused. "We have an appointment tomorrow. They sent Zach's tissue to another expert to confirm the diagnosis. Tomorrow they will have the complete pathology report and explain the best treatment options. He will likely have to undergo chemotherapy. It will be a long and difficult road." The pastor stood up. "We want to pray for you." While the group gathered around them, Lisa said, "We are so afraid." Her voice broke and the tears flowed again. And then, people they had known for only a few minutes laid their hands on little Zach and prayed as if they loved him as much as they did. Lisa felt the love of a compassionate Savior who truly understood her deep pain. Jason felt a huge burden lift off his shoulders. He couldn't protect his son. He couldn't control the outcome. But he could trust his heavenly Father to do both. Both of them left feeling an indescribable peace. For the first night in weeks, they slept.

Jason and Lisa waited in the exam room in silence, not knowing what to expect. Zach was busy playing with some toys Lisa had brought. The door opened, and they tensed up in their seats. The first words out of the doctor's mouth were "I have good news." Her heart jumped. After reviewing all the reports, they concluded Zach's cancer was *not* the aggressive type. Instead of starting chemotherapy immediately, he wanted to wait six weeks to see if the spot still showing on one of his lungs had changed. As they drove home from the appointment, tears ran down Lisa's face. God had heard their prayers and given them six wonderful weeks with their son where he could play and be a normal little boy.

Six weeks later, there was a tiny spot showing on Zach's other lung. But the doctor didn't seem too alarmed. Another six weeks. Watch and wait, Lisa heard from other parents. She waited for the next scan, trying to live a normal life in between the scans and appointments, not knowing the news each scan would bring. She watched Zach sleep so peacefully and struggled to fight back the anger. She wanted to scream at the unfairness of it all. Whenever she felt that way, God would gently touch her. A song on the radio. A Bible verse that would jump off the page. A call or note from a friend. The prayer meetings. A reminder that He hadn't forgotten them. That He was faithful.

This pattern continued. Six weeks, then three months. Then six-month and one-year intervals. Each time, there were no significant changes. And each time, they were extremely thankful. Sometimes she would forget all this was happening to them. Life felt normal, like it should feel with a growing little toddler in the house. And then she would be reminded. They had connected with other families facing the same battle. One little boy on watch and wait, just like Zach. Another who had months of chemotherapy and a surgery to remove a portion of his lung, but now the cancer was growing rapidly and had metastasized to his brain. Their hearts ached for this family. And with each appointment, it lingered at the back of their minds.

Three years passed. They were used to good checkups. But not this time. One of the two spots the doctor had been watching on Zach's lung had doubled in size. The doctors recommended surgery to remove it. "We want to stay ahead of this thing," the doctor explained. Otherwise, this nonaggressive form of cancer could develop into a more aggressive type and be far more difficult to treat. They should be able to complete the surgery via scope. Much less invasive and better for a mother's heart.

The big day arrived. They were bathed in prayer. They had prepared little Zach for what would happen. He was happy and oblivious to their concerns. He was no stranger to hospitals. They kissed him good-bye and made their way to the waiting room. They were no strangers to waiting. Only this time, they didn't wait long. No sooner had they prayed together and made themselves comfortable when Lisa's heart stopped—the surgeons entered the waiting area. *It's too soon.* But the doctor quickly dispelled their fears. They had searched. And searched some more. But all they could find inside little Zach was pink, healthy lung tissue. Nothing that resembled the growth they intended to remove. Absolutely nothing. Months passed, then years. Today, Zach is a healthy, robust big brother. His parents continue to worship a faithful God who answers prayer. A God who restores life. A God who heals.

# Even Evil Spirits Obey

*"What sort of new teaching is this?" they asked excitedly.*
*"It has such authority! Even evil spirits obey his orders!"*
MARK 1:27

She must see Him. He was in Perea teaching at the synagogue. The pain was especially intense today. *It would be easier to stay home. Better to just rest.* But something else inside her compelled her to go. Besides, she had grown used to the pain. Her deformity was part of her now. For as long as she could remember, she had been bent double. The pain had come suddenly. *When?* She thought for a moment, calculating the time. It was eighteen years ago. She woke up one morning with stiff joints and pain in her lower back. She remembered how leaning forward helped to relieve the pain. As the insidious pain continued, she continued to compensate by leaning forward. Eventually, her spine froze permanently, making it virtually impossible to stand up straight. *Yes, I must go.*

When she arrived at the synagogue, she made her way toward the women's gallery. She was thankful for an empty seat on the first row. Climbing had become nearly impossible. When Jesus stood up to teach, He immediately noticed her. Her bent posture forced her eyes to look upward at Him. She squirmed as He studied her for a moment. He seemed to know something about her even she didn't know. Then He called her over. She slowly moved toward Him, her eyes continuing to strain upward. In a gentle but commanding voice, He proclaimed, "Dear woman, you are healed of your sickness!" Then He touched her. She felt His power move directly to her spine, loosing and freeing bone and cartilage that had held her captive for years. Instantly, she could stand straight. And, oh, how she praised God! She was healed and set free (Luke 13:12–13)!

Early in His ministry, Jesus commanded an evil spirit out of a man in Capernaum and amazed the crowd by His teaching and authority. Even the evil spirits obeyed Him! Near Caesarea Philippi, He commanded an evil spirit causing deafness and muteness to come out of a child and never come back (Mark 9:25). Throughout His ministry, He went around healing all who were under the power of the devil (Acts 10:38). Now, in the final months of His ministry, He responded with compassion to this woman who suffered for eighteen years from a form of arthritis caused by an evil spirit (Luke 13:11).

That Satan would attack people and cause physical illness should come as no surprise. Scripture warns us to be alert because our great enemy, the devil, prowls around like a roaring lion looking for someone to devour (1 Peter 5:8). But not all physical or mental illness is caused by a direct attack from Satan. There are many causes of sickness in our fallen world. Certain diseases have an organic cause, physiological change to some tissue or organ of the body. We can fall sick by contacting the source of an infectious disease. Malnutrition causes illness and death in many Third World countries throughout the world, and even in parts of the West. For many, a compromised immune system due to fatigue, burnout, or failure to care for our bodies contributes to poor health. Whatever the direct cause of illness, Satan is the original source of all disease, because he is the source of all evil (John 10:10). He brought sin into the world in the garden, and sickness and disease came along with it.

But Jesus came with good news! He has power and

authority over *all* things (Matthew 28:18). Just one touch from Him restored what the enemy had stolen from this woman for eighteen long years. And He gave us the same authority to cast out demons and heal diseases in His name (John 14:12). Whatever enemy you face today in your journey toward wellness, whatever power the enemy has used against you, Jesus is *more* powerful. Whatever lies he has told you about your prognosis, Jesus is the truth. No matter how long you have suffered, Jesus has the final authority. Even evil spirits obey Him.

## Prayer

*Lord, thank You that You are a God of compassion and Your heart's desire is to set me free. Lord, You have the final authority over sickness and disease. The enemy may have plotted against me, but You have the power to destroy his evil plans. You have the power to make me whole. If there is a spirit at the root of my illness, I command it to go now in the name of Jesus and never come back!*

*Lord, thank You that You are more powerful than the enemy. In Your name, I reclaim everything he has stolen from me! I praise You, Lord, for the victory You have won for me! I am more than a conqueror in You (Romans 8:37). I love You, Lord.*

# A Grateful Heart

*When Jesus arrived at Peter's house, Peter's mother-in-law was sick in bed with a high fever. But when Jesus touched her hand, the fever left her. Then she got up and prepared a meal for him.*
MATHEW 8:14–15

*They should be coming soon. Service will be over. They will be hungry. Must get up.* She tried to lift herself out of bed, but her head throbbed. Sweat covered her face and neck, her wet hair matted to her head. Hot, so hot. Her body shook with chills. She pulled up the blanket and then abruptly threw it off. The room spun around her. She was losing her mind. *Need to get up. They will be hungry.* In a moment of clarity, the reality of her situation struck. *I'm dying. This is what dying feels like.* Through a blur, she saw someone standing at her bedside. Someone touched her hand. The confusion began to lift. A refreshing cool sensation washed over her body. Relief. Her eyes focused, and she found herself looking into the face of pure love. It was the Teacher. "You must be hungry," she said. Before He could answer, she got out of bed and began preparing a meal.

Her hands busy kneading dough, she thought about how her life had changed. She was alone, but she had opened her home to them. Her daughter's husband, Peter, and his brother Andrew needed a place to stay while in Capernaum. They were from nearby Bethsaida, but after the Teacher called them, they needed to be here with Him. Oh, how she loved serving them. Somehow, she knew she was part of something important. Somehow, she knew His love would change the world (Matthew 8:14–17; Mark 1:29–34; Luke 4:38–41).

Three Gospel writers record the healing of Peter's mother-in-law, and Jesus used a slightly different method in each. In Matthew, He touched her hand (Matthew 8:15). Luke wrote that Jesus "rebuked the fever" (Luke 4:39). Mark records that He "took her by the hand, and helped her sit up" (Mark 1:31). It was likely a combination of words and touch that healed her. Regardless of His method, Jesus acted without delay when He learned of her illness (Mark 1:30). He never ignored an opportunity to meet the needs of those who were suffering because He cares deeply about every single person.

Later that evening, Jesus further demonstrated to His disciples His compassion for the sick and hurting. With the whole town gathered at the door to watch (Mark 1:33), He cast out evil spirits with a simple command and healed all the sick people who came to Him (Matthew 8:16). In doing so, He not only met their immediate needs but fulfilled the word of the Lord through the prophet Isaiah, who said, "He took our sicknesses and removed our diseases" (Matthew 8:17). Since this verse substitutes "sicknesses" and "diseases" for the words "weaknesses" and "sorrows" in Isaiah 53:4, we can know He included physical healing when Isaiah said, "He was whipped so we could be healed" (Isaiah 53:5).

Peter's mother-in-law was bedridden and close to death, but the words and touch of Jesus were all it took to pull her to her feet. Her first response to receiving His love was to give it back. She served Him and those staying in her home with a heart of gratitude. Jesus feels the same love and compassion for you. He will never ignore you. He may not heal in the way you expect, but He always heals. You matter to Him. He was whipped to prove how much you matter. How else can you respond to such love but with a grateful heart?

# Prayer

*Forgive me for believing the lie that You don't care about me and that You have somehow forgotten about me. I know it is virtually impossible for You to forget me. Yes, Lord, You know my every need. I can trust You won't delay. You proved Your love for me once and for all on the cross where You said, "It is finished." You paid the price and made Your love for me complete. I am overwhelmed by the width, length, height, and depth of Your love (Ephesians 3:18). It humbles me.*

*Thank You, Lord, that I am healed by Your stripes! Rivers of gratitude overflow from my heart. I can't help but give it all back to You, Lord. What else can I do? Show me who needs Your love and compassion today. Help me give Your love away. As I pour out Your love, may You continue to heal, restore, refill, and replenish. More, Lord, more. I love You.*

# Set Free

*For God has not given us a spirit of fear and timidity,*
*but of power, love, and self-discipline.*
2 TIMOTHY 1:7

Jan was recently diagnosed with early stage breast cancer. Her doctor recommended either a lumpectomy to remove the lump or, if she preferred, a total mastectomy. It was her choice. He sent her home with resources explaining both surgical options and referrals to an oncologist and plastic surgeon. He told her to take her time. There was no immediate rush to decide. But Jan viewed things differently. "I just want this cancer off me. I want it off me *now*! He can take off both breasts so it can't come back!" she cried to her friend.

Three years later, she waited for the doctor in the exam room, her knuckles white from gripping the arms of the chair and her heart beating out of her chest. She hated these appointments. They would take her blood, poke and prod, shuffle their papers, and take their time. Then the doctor would look at her with "the verdict." Either she was "well" until the next checkup, or. . . Her mind raced. *Those headaches I've been having. Maybe the cancer is back?* Her lower back hurt last week for a few days, and she couldn't help but wonder why. *When will this nightmare be over? Am I really healed, or am I just a walking time bomb waiting for cancer to implode throughout my body? I can't live this way.*

No, she can't. But unfortunately, fear is holding her captive. She is afraid of the unknown, afraid that bad things will happen, and ultimately, afraid for her life. There is a reason the acronym for fear is False Evidence Appearing

Real. When fear controls us, we become chronic worriers or control freaks. We can suffer real physical symptoms, such as anxiety and panic attacks. Living in a constant "fight or flight" mode can take a huge toll on our health. Fear can drive us to hunker down in isolation, cutting ourselves off from a world that might harm us. The most dangerous by-product of fear is unbelief. If we don't believe we are healed, we don't have to fear what we believe won't happen. Fear can drive us into a state of apathy. If we expect nothing from God, we won't be disappointed when we get nothing.

We are bound to the thing we fear. It has power and control over our lives. The only fear we should ever have is a holy, reverent fear of the Lord Himself. This kind of fear binds us to *Him* for love, provision, safety, and protection (Isaiah 8:11–14). If we fear anything other than God, Satan uses it to paralyze and torment us. He does this by drawing our attention away from God and getting us to focus on our circumstances. Then he floods our thoughts with fear-filled imaginations and possibilities. Remember, he is a liar and his only purpose is to steal, kill, and destroy (John 10:10).

Fear is always a trust issue. Do we trust in the goodness of God and His promises or not? If Satan can get us to stop trusting God and to doubt His willingness and power to handle our problems, he can hold us captive to fear.

When fear controls us, it robs us of our joy, our peace, and our hope. It encourages us to grumble, complain, and get angry. But fear can only control us when we make the choice to come into agreement with its lies.

Jan made a major decision while paralyzed with fear. We should be careful to make no major decisions out of fear because God is not in the midst of those decisions. The Bible is clear that fear does *not* come from Him. As a believer, your old self has died, so fear is dead. You are a new creation, united with Christ. In Him you can have power, love, and a sound mind. His perfect love alone casts out all fear (1 John 4:18). Fear simply cannot coexist with His love. If fear is holding you captive, you can choose to hang on to your fears and anxieties, or you can renounce them and send them to the foot of the cross. You can be set free.

## Prayer

*When David was tormented with fear, he laid it all out before You and then he trusted You (Psalm 143). Lord, please reveal any fears that have been tormenting me. Let the truth of Your Word and my identity as a child of God penetrate the deepest place of my heart and bring revelation, comfort, peace, and freedom. Lord, help my faith in You to completely displace all my fear and unbelief.*

*Lord, I receive Your perfect love. Forgive me for allowing fear to torment me. I'm sorry for doubting Your goodness and Your faithfulness to provide for my every need. Lord, in Your name, I confess and cast out all my fears. By Your grace, help me not to lean on my own understanding but to trust You in all Your ways.*

# He Has Overcome

*"I have told you all this so that you may have peace in me.*
*Here on earth you will have many trials and sorrows.*
*But take heart, because I have overcome the world."*
JOHN 16:33

Katy and Brad heard about the healing room from a family member. They drove more than forty miles through snow and rush-hour traffic to get there. Katy was diagnosed several months ago with amyotrophic lateral sclerosis (ALS), also known as Lou Gehrig's disease, and it was progressing fast. Her left side was growing weaker. She was losing feeling in her left hand, arm, and leg. Recently, she started walking with a limp. Upon hearing her story, a group of prayer ministers gathered around and prayed. They anointed her with oil. She felt a strong outpouring of the Lord's presence. She felt His peace. She clearly received His love. But as they prayed, Brad grew more and more agitated. One of the prayer ministers looked directly at him. "How are you doing?" Brad shook his head back and forth. Not good. He fought back tears and finally spoke. "It's not fair. She is the kindest, most selfless person I know. She has served the Lord all her life. She feeds the homeless. She is a giver, and she has great faith. It's just not fair."

Our limited human minds just can't understand when bad things happen to good people. We're much less conflicted when bad things happen to bad people! But it's imperative to know that no one is sitting up in heaven keeping score. We can never "earn" our way into God's favor by doing good. No, it's all about what's been *done* for us. Jesus died because we can never do enough. We can only be made right with God by believing Jesus died to take away our sins (Romans 3:22–25). In this one ultimate act of unconditional love, God wiped our slate clean. As His children, we are saved by grace, a free gift to all who believe, so none can boast or outgive the other (Ephesians 2:8–9).

Like many of us, Brad struggled to accept that God's favor doesn't depend on how good we are or how many kind things we've done. Even the world's worst sinner cannot escape the Lord's outstretched arms of grace if he is truly repentant. Only by trusting what God has done for you at the cross will you be whole and perfect in His sight (Ephesians 2:8–10). It's only by this grace that we receive every blessing in our lives. And it's only by His mercy that we aren't penalized for every sin.

While Jesus came to save the world, the enemy's purpose is to steal, kill, and destroy (John 10:10). He is a liar and a deceiver, and his goal is to demoralize you and make you cower in intimidation (1 Peter 5:8). Being a good Christian doesn't guarantee a trouble-free life, because your enemy the devil doesn't play fair! Even Jesus was spat upon, beaten, misunderstood, betrayed, and crucified. But His sacrifice guarantees you direct access to the throne room of God and a supernatural storehouse of peace in the midst of all your trials and sorrows. You can be pressed on every side by troubles, but He promises you will never be crushed and broken. You may fall down, but you will get up again and keep on going (2 Corinthians 4:8–9). The Lord Himself is fighting for you (Joshua 23:10; Exodus 14:25), and He will never, ever abandon you (Hebrews 13:5).

That night, the Lord began to restore Katy. She felt strength return to her leg and arm, walked without a limp, and slept on her left side without pain and numbness. You, too, can take heart, because your God is a restoration expert. No matter what the enemy destroys, He can gather up the broken pieces and make all things work together for good according to *His* purposes for those who love Him (Romans 8:28). He restored His fallen Kingdom (Amos 9:11), He fulfilled the promise in Christ's resurrection (Acts 15:16–17), and He removed your sin and restored you to Himself. He can redeem all that the enemy has stolen, and *then* some (1 Samuel 30:8; Job 42:10). No, the devil doesn't play fair. But *God* has overcome the world.

## Prayer

*Father, forgive me for believing I could ever earn Your favor or that my goodness could somehow pay the price for my healing. You already paid, Lord. You paid the price with Your blood. There is nothing more I have to do, except receive Your gift of love. Lord, I receive Your grace, Your mercy, and Your forgiveness. I receive Your perfect peace.*

*Lord, thank You that You fight my battle for me and You will never leave me or forsake me. In Your name, and by Your authority, I take back everything the enemy has stolen from me! You are good, Lord. All that is broken in my life You can heal and restore. You can pick up the pieces of my failing health and make me whole again! Restore me, Lord! Thank You for your promise of redemption and for making all things work together for good, according to Your purposes. Praise Jesus, You have overcome the world!*

# The Secret to Answered Prayer

*"If you abide in Me, and My words abide in you,
you will ask what you desire, and it shall be done for you."*

JOHN 15:7 NKJV

Mary was working hard competing for a promotion she desperately wanted at work. She didn't have time anymore for her small group Bible study. Even her prayer life had gone cold. Now, her health suffered serious consequences. She didn't have time to be sick, and God just wasn't listening to her prayers.

John grew up in the church, but over the years, he drifted away. Now, he was hospitalized for a serious work injury that could leave him paralyzed. "How can I ask God for anything?" John asked the pastor who had come to pray. "I haven't been paying much attention to God. Why should He answer my prayers now?"

Jolene was a volunteer in her church where the actions of a few leaders left her deeply wounded. She pulled away from all the ministries she had been serving. She pulled away from the weekend services and her prayer group. She felt angry, betrayed, and alone. *What do You want from me, God?* Nothing but silence.

Jesus gives us the secret to answered prayer: "abiding." Abiding means to stay, dwell, and remain in His presence and to live from an intimate connection with God. When you became a believer, the Holy Spirit took up residence in your spirit. He abides in you. But abiding is a two-way street. The Lord abides in *relationship* with us. We abide in *fellowship* with Him.

Jesus established your relationship with the Father through His death and resurrection. Your faith in Him allows you to come boldly and confidently into His presence (Ephesians 3:12). Your relationship with God is never in doubt. It can never be broken, regardless of anything you might do or experience (Hebrews 13:5; Romans 8:38–39). This relationship is based on your identity in Christ. You are a child of God ( John 1:12), justified by faith (Romans 5:1), making you a citizen of heaven where Jesus lives and reigns (Philippians 3:20). Your citizenship can never be revoked because God never changes (Hebrews 13:8).

But unlike our unchanging relationship with God, our fellowship with Him *can* change. Many factors can cause us to drift out of fellowship. Mary let the cares of this world distract her until they displaced her devotion to God (Matthew 13:20). John believed the lie that his actions made him unlovable and unworthy of God's grace, and his injury was God's way of punishment (Ephesians 2:4–8). Jolene let past wounds and offenses turn into bitterness that held her captive to the sin of unforgiveness (Mark 11:24–25). All three had drifted out of fellowship, cutting them off from intimacy with the Father and hindering their prayer lives.

But Jesus showed us through the parable of the prodigal son just how quickly our Father will restore fellowship. After squandering all his inheritance on wild living, this son was so poor and hungry that he was forced to eat with the pigs. Pigs were unclean according to Moses' law, so he had truly sunk to the depths of humiliation. When he came to his senses, he returned home to his father, who ran to him with open arms and threw a party to celebrate his return (Luke 15:22–24).

This young rebellious son wanted to be free and live as he pleased. He had to hit rock bottom to come back home.

Abiding in your heavenly Father is very much the same. He will give you plenty of opportunities to fellowship with Him, but He won't force it. You might have to experience a crisis to look to Him for help. But your Father is full of love and patience. When you humble yourself before Him and come back into fellowship, He welcomes you home with open arms, no matter how long you've been gone. Your Father wants to bless you, and He knows everything flows from that place of abiding. In that place of intimacy, you hear His voice. Your heart beats with His. Your prayers are His prayers. He abides in you, and you abide in Him—the secret to answered prayer.

## Prayer

*Father, thank You that everything flows out of intimacy with You. All the promises and blessings I so desperately want; whether it's guidance, direction, peace, provision, or healing, all these things flow from Your presence because You ARE these things. If I have You, I have everything I need (Matthew 6:33). You are the Lord, the I AM (Exodus 3:14). You are the God who heals.*

*Lord, teach me to abide. Help me to stay in fellowship with You around the clock. Forgive me for letting the world distract me from fellowship with You. Please reveal any sin that is blocking my intimacy with You, keeping me from fellowship, or hindering my prayer life. Reveal any lies I have believed about myself or Your character. Forgive me, Lord! Show me Your truth! I want to know You, Lord. I want to know Your heart. I want Your prayers to be my prayers. I want to abide in Your presence, the place of answered prayer. I want to abide always.*

# Jehovah-Rapha: Al's Story

Al had a long, successful career in sales and business development. Shortly after his sixtieth birthday, he was let go from a job he loved. He didn't worry. After a short hiatus, he was hired by another company that needed his expertise. The first year, things went okay. He was getting established while helping the company figure out its value proposition and positioning in the marketplace. The second year was a disaster. It started with a long, cold, dreary winter. At first he thought it was Seasonal Affective Disorder (SAD). The sun didn't shine for days on end and the subzero temperatures kept him locked up in the prison of his home office. *Cabin fever.* Yes, it must be SAD because that's surely how he felt.

He kept working hard. It was a long, arduous sales cycle. He would get a prospect up to the point of a sale, and then the sale wouldn't close. Time after time, over and over again, no matter what he did, no matter how hard he worked, the sales didn't come. By the time the snow melted, he had never felt so miserable.

But with spring came home projects. He poured himself into one project after another. One particularly mammoth project took several weeks, requiring him to work every single night to complete it. He was focused and driven. Anything to achieve something, to see some reward for his efforts. When he finally finished, he thought he would feel great joy and satisfaction. Instead, he tumbled into a deep, dark pit of despair. His head pounded. He lay on the couch and could barely function. A sales guy who always enjoyed people didn't want anything to do with them. He was tired and irritable. He barely talked to his family. He felt trapped. No matter how hard he tried, he couldn't pull himself back into the light.

The final blow came during his semiannual performance review at work. He didn't achieve his goals. The sales weren't there. The words jumped off the page his boss put in front of him. *Does not meet expectations.* He snapped. He could not logically discuss the barriers he encountered, the problems inherent in the business model, or the unrealistic sales goals that didn't match the market potential. Instead, he simply offered to quit. But the boss didn't want his resignation. Instead, he put him on a performance improvement plan, the first he had ever been on in his entire career.

He tumbled further and further into the dark, hopeless pit. *There must be something terribly wrong. This is not me. I don't even recognize myself.* The pounding headache finally drove him to the doctor—that, and the darkness that held him captive. The doctor ordered an MRI and a battery of tests. He was convinced she would find something, but his test results were normal. She was gentle and thorough. She diagnosed situational depression and anxiety disorder and recommended an antidepressant and close follow-up. He struggled with the stigma of taking drugs. But he was desperate to find himself again.

As the weeks passed, he began to cope again. To pray. To hear God again. He continued the medication along with some inner healing ministry. With his pastor facilitating, God revealed that his identity had been tied to his own achievement and success instead of Christ. When he couldn't achieve, he felt worthless. He didn't like himself. How could God possibly like him? The

Lord probed deep to uncover his childhood roots—where he first started believing the lie that he wasn't valuable or loved unless he achieved. The Holy Spirit replaced those lies with the truth of how the Father sees him as His beloved son.

Several more weeks passed, and gradually the darkness lifted. The Lord reached out His nail-scarred hand, and Al grabbed it. He pulled him out of the pit and set his feet on solid ground. There were still problems at work, but he could cope. There was still much uncertainty ahead, but he could be certain of a faithful God who would never fail him. Al marked his healing and newfound freedom in a special way. While in Israel on Yom Kippur (Jewish New Year), he hiked through the same Judean wilderness where Jesus spent forty days being tempted by Satan. Then he celebrated the victory he shared with his Lord by being rebaptized in the Jordan River. He rose out of the water with both arms raised, praising the God of new beginnings: Jehovah-Rapha, the God who heals.

# One Thing

*"I don't know whether he is a sinner," the man replied.*
*"But I know this: I was blind, and now I can see!"*
JOHN 9:25

Jesus and His disciples were in Jerusalem for the feast. They'd just left the temple, and he knew they were talking about *him* and the cause of his blindness. "Rabbi, who sinned, this man or his parents, that he was born blind?" Suffering was thought to be a result of sin in their culture, but as the one born blind, he never thought this logic made sense. Many sinned, but not everyone was born blind as a result! Jesus' answer surprised him. "It was not because of his sins or his parents' sins. This happened so the power of God could be seen in him."

What happened next astonished him more. He could sense someone moving toward him. He felt a warm sensation surround him. It was strangely peaceful. He sensed the person bending over and then heard a familiar sound. *Ptuh.* Spitting? He flinched a bit when he felt the hands begin to smear something cool and wet on both of his eyes. It smelled like dirt. *Mud.* He knew it was Jesus. "Go wash in the Pool of Siloam," He told him. Not quite sure what to expect, the blind man obediently made his way south to the pool.

It took him a few minutes to get there. He begged on these streets and knew them well. On the way, he dared not hope. Jesus usually healed instantly. *Could it be?* Arriving at the ritual pool, he quickly took his clothes off and stepped in, each step down taking him deeper into the water. Cupping the water in his hands, he began washing the dried mud off his closed eyelids. Even before he opened his eyes, he could see the light. Slowly, ever so slowly, his squinting eyes grew accustomed to the bright sunlight reflecting off the water. Both arms shot up in wonder as he beheld his first view of the world outside of his imagination. *I can see. Praise Jesus, I can really see!* He ran to tell his neighbors the good news, how Jesus put mud on his eyes and restored his sight.

To his surprise, those who knew him before were skeptical. He had to convince them he really was the same blind man who sat and begged by the temple. "I am the man!" he insisted. And he told them about Jesus, the mud, and washing in the pool. Unconvinced, they brought him to the Pharisees, who demanded an explanation. He told them how Jesus healed him. "He is a prophet," he said confidently. But the religious leaders insisted that Jesus could not be of God because He broke the law and healed on the Sabbath. Then they tried to discredit his claim of blindness by demanding the "real" truth from his parents. Fearing retaliation, his parents simply said, "He is of age; ask him."

And again, they asked him. They even accused Jesus of being a sinner. Exasperated by their refusal to believe him, he insisted that only a man from God could heal the eyes of a blind man. He didn't know any answers to the questions they asked. He didn't need to know. He only knew one thing: "I was blind but now I see!" They hurled insults at him and argued about where Jesus came from. But he wasn't afraid of them. And he got the last word. "God does not listen to sinners. He listens to the godly person who does his will. Nobody has ever heard of opening the eyes of a man born blind. If this man were not from God, he could do nothing." And with that, they threw him out of the temple for good (John 9:1–34 NIV).

This man heard the same frustrating questions over and over. He didn't understand why or even how he was healed, and he didn't care. He just knew he was blind, but now he could see. And he knew the One to praise for his radically changed life, the One whose power could now be seen in him. He believed and worshipped Jesus (John 9:36–38).

In your own healing journey, people may be wondering why the world has been so unfair to you. They watch as you walk to your pool of Siloam, and they see you emerge from the pool with your life transformed. Regardless of your circumstances or the nature of your journey, God can use it to demonstrate His power and bring glory to His Son. And in the midst of all the questions, only one thing truly matters. Only His power can change your life forever.

## Prayer

*Lord, I don't understand all the reasons for my sickness or the methods and timing You use to heal and restore. But the one thing I DO know is that You have the power to change my life forever. You are Jesus, the Messiah, the One sent from heaven, my Redeemer. You alone have the power to save and heal. Lord, as I walk out my healing journey and emerge from my pool of Siloam, let Your grace and Your goodness be seen through me. I worship You, Lord!*

*Thank You for Your promise that everything works together for the good of those who love You (Romans 8:28). I believe in Your ability to heal and restore. Please, Lord, change me. Use my life for Your glory! Let Your mighty works be on display through me. Help me tell the world of Your radical life-changing power!*

# Just Do It

*So Naaman went down to the Jordan River and dipped himself*
*seven times, as the man of God had instructed him. And his skin*
*became as healthy as the skin of a young child, and he was healed!*
2 KINGS 5:14

Naaman stood with his horses and chariots waiting at the door of Elisha's house. He was a war hero, the commander of King Aram's army. His king had great admiration for him because of the great victories he had won. This prophet of Israel would surely come to him and heal him of his leprosy. His wife's servant girl from Israel had said so. His king had as much as ordered it so by writing the letter to the king of Israel. The letter said, "With this letter I present my servant Naaman. I want you to heal him of his leprosy." And here he was, waiting to be healed.

He started out from Syria carrying the letter along with 750 pounds of silver, 150 pounds of gold, and 10 sets of clothing. It should be more than enough to ensure it done. He had presented the letter to the king of Israel, who sent him directly to the prophet's house. And now he was growing impatient. He shuffled his feet back and forth. Surely this prophet would have come to meet him by now. The door opened, and someone emerged from the house. *Finally. Is it the prophet?* No, the man had come to deliver a message from Elisha. Before he could object, the messenger said, "Go and wash yourself seven times in the Jordan River. Then your skin will be restored, and you will be healed of your leprosy."

*What? Wash in that filthy river?* He was livid. "I thought

he would certainly come out to meet me!" he said. "I expected him to wave his hand over the leprosy and call on the name of the LORD his God and heal me! Aren't the rivers of Damascus, the Abana and the Pharpar, better than any of the rivers of Israel? Why shouldn't I wash in them and be healed?" He stalked away in a rage.

Following after him, his officers tried to reason with him. If the prophet had told him to do something very difficult, he would have done it without question. So why wouldn't he obey something very simple like go wash and be cured? Conceding to their rationale, he went down to the bank of the Jordan River. He looked at the murky water, wondering what in the world he was thinking. Feeling foolish, he sighed, undressed, and dipped his body seven times as the prophet instructed. After the seventh time, he looked at his skin and couldn't believe his eyes. It was as healthy as that of a young child. *Praise the God of Israel! I am healed!* He quickly dressed and ran with his officers to find the prophet. Standing before him, he lowered his head in reverence and said, "Now I know that there is no God in all the world except in Israel" (2 Kings 5:1–19).

Naaman was a great warrior, and he expected royal treatment. But God expected obedience. Obedience begins with humility, and believing God's way is better than our own way, even if we don't understand it. Naaman had to humble himself and obey God's instructions before he could get well. Sometimes we simply have to move out in faithful obedience, even if it makes no sense. Washing in the Jordan seven times made no sense to Naaman. It wasn't logical. He expected Elisha to greet him personally, wave a hand over his leprosy, and call on his God to heal. But God doesn't submit to our human logic, and healing doesn't always come in the way we expect. God has His own agenda. Naaman acknowledged the one true God as a result of his miracle. And he likely told many people about the power of the God of Israel when he returned home.

Is God waiting for your obedience? God speaks into your spirit and makes His instructions known in the scriptures. We're disobedient when we know what to do and don't do it. As you read His Word and listen to His voice, He may ask you to do things you don't want to do, like dip seven times in a muddy river. Don't let your pride and self-will hinder God's blessing. Think back to the last thing you knew you should do, that thing you left undone that nags in your spirit and won't go away. The next time He prompts you, just do it!

## Prayer

*Lord, show me where I have been disobedient to You. Reveal to me any areas where my pride and self-will have hindered my blessing. Forgive me if I've allowed the concerns of this world to distract me from following Your leading (Matthew 8:21). Forgive me when I've had good intentions but failed to act (Matthew 21:28–31). Forgive me when I thought my own good works could substitute for Your clear directions (1 Samuel 15:22).*

*Lord, help me to be obedient to You, especially when I don't understand. Your ways are higher than my ways (Isaiah 55:9). I want to know You, Lord. I want to hear Your voice. When I hear Your prompting, I don't want to doubt or hesitate. I want to just do it.*

# He Dwells in Your Praises

*Yet you are holy, enthroned on the praises of Israel.*
PSALM 22:3

When King Jehoshaphat heard that the armies of Moab, Ammon, and Mount Seir were mounting an attack against him, he cried out for God to rescue the people. As the mighty army approached, God sent word that the people should not be afraid. The battle was not theirs, but His, and they would not even need to fight! The next day, the king appointed singers to walk ahead of the army to sing and give praise to the Lord. At the sound of their voices, the Lord set the enemy armies into confusion, and they fought against one another. Not a single one escaped, and not a single Israelite was killed. There was so much equipment, clothing, and other valuables that it took the people three days to collect all the plunder. On the fourth day, they gathered in the Valley of Blessing to praise and thank the Lord for their victory (2 Chronicles 20:10–26).

Nearly a thousand years later, the apostle Paul and Silas were thrown into a jail in Macedonia for preaching the Gospel and casting out a demon from a fortune-teller who earned a lot of money for her masters. They were severely beaten with wooden rods and placed in stocks in an inner dungeon cell to make sure they wouldn't escape. Around midnight they were praying and singing hymns to God as the other prisoners listened. Suddenly, there was a massive earthquake, and the prison was shaken to its foundations. All the doors immediately flew open, and the chains of every prisoner fell off! The jailer who was charged to guard them panicked, fearing for his life when he woke up to see the prison doors wide open. But Paul and Silas shared the Gospel with him, and he and his entire household were saved (Acts 16:16–34).

Some days, your battle against sickness may feel like a mighty army is marching against you, leaving you little chance of victory. You may feel imprisoned, bound in chains with no hope of escape. When you are fighting for your life, singing hymns and praises to the Lord may not be the first thing on your mind. You may be more inclined to use all the worldly weapons at your disposal to fight back. Or you might simply want to sit in your chains and give up. But praise is the most powerful weapon you have at your disposal when the enemy attacks.

Expressing your love, adoration, and sincere devotion to God through praise can push the darkness out of your circumstances. God does not dwell in the darkness. He is not found in your sickness. He dwells in your praises. Glorifying His name and lifting Him high in praise and worship literally changes the atmosphere. His presence was so powerful in the singers of Jehoshaphat's army that it scattered the enemy and rendered them ineffective. It was so powerful in the praises of Paul and Silas that it shook the prison to its foundations and set the prisoners free. Praise sets the enemy running because he can't dwell in the presence of the Lord. He has no choice but to flee (James 4:7). Praise is an exclamation of your faith and a declaration that you fight from a place of victory. And your victory is assured in Christ (Romans 8:37).

Your battle for health and wellness is His battle, not yours. It doesn't even belong to your doctors. Send your praises ahead of the battle. Sing hymns of praise in your prison of sickness. Put on the praise music, go find a Spirit-filled worship service, and shout your praises to the Lord! Watch the enemy scatter in confusion. Watch the chains fall off and the prison doors open. The enemy may have formed an army against you, but His Son already defeated it for you at the cross. You don't have to wait until the battle is over to start celebrating. Send your praises on ahead, and soon that valley of sickness and disease will become your Valley of Blessing. All because He dwells in your praises.

## Prayer

*Lord, a vast army marches against me! I cry out for You to rescue me. I am held captive in this prison of sickness and despair. I can't escape these chains. But I praise You, Lord! I sing praises to Your holy name! I love You, Lord. I worship You. I lift Your name on high.*

*Lord, this battle belongs to You alone. At the sound of Your name, the enemy has no choice but to flee. As I sing Your praises, may the enemy of my health and wellness turn on itself and be utterly destroyed. As I sing hymns of joy, shake the foundation of all that holds me captive! Release my chains, Lord. Open the doors of this prison of sickness and set me free! Thank You that I am victorious in You, Lord. I sing alleluia in my Valley of Blessing, because Your presence dwells in my praises!*

# From the Overflow

*Soon afterward Jesus began a tour of the nearby towns and villages,
preaching and announcing the Good News about the Kingdom of God.
He took his twelve disciples with him, along with some women who
had been cured of evil spirits and diseases. Among them were
Mary Magdalene, from whom he had cast out seven demons.*

LUKE 8:1–2

She was Mary from Magdala, a prosperous fishing village
located on the northwest side of the Sea of Galilee. A
woman of high standing, she lived comfortably, except for
one thing—the insanity that held her captive. She had always
been anxious and nervous. The fits would come and go. When
they came, they left her helplessly out of control. She would
shake and thrash violently, harming herself and anyone who
got close to her. Until she met Him. When He looked at
her, He didn't see a deranged, wild-eyed woman with sunken
cheeks and unkempt hair. He saw the woman God created,
a devoted disciple who would soon be a blessing to Him and
many others. He commanded seven tormenting demons to
come out that day and to never come back. Immediately,
her mind cleared and her sanity returned. Her countenance
was completely restored, and she was free from a lifetime of
darkness and oppression.

Overwhelmed with gratitude, she left her home to follow
Him along with Joanna, Susanna, and the others. They went
with Him as He traveled from place to place, preaching and
teaching the good news of the Kingdom. She ministered to
Him and contributed her own resources toward His mission.
She was with Him through it all, and unlike His disciples, she

was with Him faithfully until the end. She was there when He was arrested and put on trial. She was there when Pontius Pilate announced His death sentence to the bloodthirsty crowd. She watched as He was whipped, mocked, spat on, and brutally beaten beyond recognition. She followed as He stumbled through the streets dragging His cross up the hill. She winced at every strike as the nails were driven into His hands and feet. She watched from a distance as He hung dying on the cross, His every agonizing cry piercing her broken heart. She was there when He took His final breath, and she followed as they carried His body to the tomb.

How could she not? Her heart overflowed with love and pure devotion for the One who had come to save the world. She had watched Him transform one life after another. He not only restored her own physical and mental health, but also lifted her and other women out of the degrading position that they suffered in Jewish culture. Women were locked out of the synagogues and not allowed to learn from rabbis. But Jesus treated women with dignity and respect and had raised her into the joy of fellowship with the King. She traveled with Him and was one of His disciples, part of His ministry team, clearly showing that all people are equal in the eyes of God.

Mary was richly blessed by the Lord, and her service to Him overflowed from a heart of gratitude. He honored her love and devotion by allowing her to be the first witness to the resurrected Christ (John 20:14–16). Then He commissioned her to be the first evangelist, to go find His disciples and tell them the good news that He had risen and was ascending to the Father (John 20:17).

While it can be difficult to be grateful in your struggle for wellness, you can be thankful for His presence in the midst of it and for all the good He can accomplish through it. Like Mary, make a habit of sitting at His feet and spending time in His presence where He will always reveal more of His grace and goodness. As you follow Him and His Spirit pours into your heart, you can't help but love and serve Him from the overflow. In this deep place of intimacy, you will be continually strengthened, encouraged, and blessed by the power of the risen Lord.

## Prayer

*Lord, forgive me when I have focused on the challenges of my illness, forgetting to thank You for all the blessings in my life. Help me to remember that no matter how big my problems might be, You are bigger! In You, I am more than a conqueror (Romans 8:37)!*

*God, thank You that a grateful heart releases more blessing. Help me to start with the small victories in my healing journey—a good day, a good doctor report, a phone call from a thoughtful friend, or a parking place at the clinic. Thank You for Your faithfulness, Lord! My heart overflows with love and devotion for the One who came to save me! I receive Your grace and goodness. Help me to always bless others from the overflow.*

# Inside Out

*Now may the God of peace make you holy in every way,*
*and may your whole spirit and soul and body be kept*
*blameless until our Lord Jesus Christ comes again.*
1 Thessalonians 5:23

Anne suffered from chronic health problems most of her life. She was on medication for muscular pain, insomnia, severe headaches, depression, and idiopathic digestive issues. She could rarely leave home unless she was certain there would be a bathroom nearby. Recently, she complained of chest pains and a rapid heartbeat. She had always been a worrier, but her husband noticed she was increasingly anxious and frustrated with her doctors. A friend from his Bible study suggested she meet with a pastor at his church. Desperate for answers, Anne reluctantly agreed. After a year of pastoral care and inner healing ministry, Anne is symptom free and off most of her medications.

Anne learned that God created us with three parts: body, soul, and spirit. Our *body* functions and connects with the physical world. It's made up of organs and cells as well as our body systems.

Our *soul*, or "outer man," is our mind, will, and emotions. Our soul gives us our personality, and through it, we live out our relationship with God and others. Our mind is where we do our thinking and reasoning, hold our attitudes and beliefs, and experience feelings. Our will enables us to make choices.

Our *spirit*, or "inner man," gives meaning and purpose to our life and enables us to love God and others. We communicate and have fellowship with God through our spirit.

It is the eternal part of us that understands spiritual truth. When we accept Jesus, the Holy Spirit takes up residence in our human spirit and we become new persons, no longer obligated to follow our sinful nature.

Anne also learned that her body, soul, and spirit are divinely aligned and interconnected. In divine alignment, the Holy Spirit rules our spirit, the spirit rules our soul, and the soul rules our body. Our spiritual health has a significant impact on our emotional health. And since our mind, will, and emotions connect to the body through complex body systems such as our nervous and immune systems, our soul has a significant influence on our physical health. If one part of our being is not aligned with the others, our physical body systems will be upset.

We can fall out of alignment when our soul takes over and our old nature rules instead of the spirit. Living by our thoughts, desires, and emotions alone pulls us back into the world and cuts us off from God's power and promises. John showed the importance of caring for the soul as it relates to physical health when he wrote, "Beloved, I pray that you may prosper in all things and be in health, just as your soul prospers" (3 John 1:2 NKJV).

Paul said if your sinful nature controls your mind, it leads to death. But letting the Spirit control your mind leads to life and peace (Romans 8:6). Anne let her worry, fear, and anxiety go unchecked, and it eventually took a tremendous toll on her physical body. If we don't willfully trust the Spirit with our problems, we can be left feeling frustrated and powerless. We might even cope by self-medicating, further exacerbating the impact on our physical health. Instead of conforming to the thought patterns of the world, we can stay aligned by allowing God to change the way we think

(Romans 12:2). Your mind can be renewed by feeding your spirit with the promises of scripture. In this way, new thought patterns emerge that align with God's truth instead of Satan's lies, leading to healthy behaviors and habits and better outcomes. You can renew your mind each day by choosing to submit your soul to your spirit, casting your cares on Jesus, and letting God be God.

A renewed mind led by the Spirit can play a significant role in your emotional and physical health. Interestingly, when our body is sick, we tend to focus on the physical battle. But Anne and many others have found that if they first address the spiritual issues, the natural will adjust itself accordingly. The physical facts eventually catch up with the Truth. It might take some time, but you could be healed from the inside out.

## Prayer

*Lord, thank You that I am perfectly and wonderfully made. Only You could create such a complex masterpiece! Forgive me for falling out of alignment and for letting unhealthy mindsets and emotions rule over my life instead of Your Spirit within me. Forgive me for not trusting You. I cast my cares on You, Lord! Help me to hold all my thoughts captive under Your authority (2 Corinthians 10:5). Thank You for the promise that Your truth will set me free (John 8:32).*

*Lord, I speak life and peace over my body and soul. Body, submit to my soul, and soul, submit to my spirit! Renew my mind, Lord! Help me replace worry, stress, and other unhealthy thoughts, emotions, and habits with the truth of Your Word. Give me new thought patterns that align with Your truth instead of*

*Satan's lies. Every day, help me to live in the spirit instead of the flesh so I can hear Your voice, receive Your protection, and be healed from the inside out.*

## Jehovah-Rapha: Trisha's Story

She had always been this way. It was the only life
she had ever known. She was born prematurely. A
compressed umbilical cord deprived her brain of oxygen
and determined her fate: cerebral palsy (CP). It was a
milder case, leaving her unable to control the muscles
in her left leg and causing abnormal stiffness, impaired
movement, and coordination problems that impacted
her gait. While she could walk unassisted, she often
used a cane or walker for balance and safety. She took it
all in stride. *It is what it is*, she reasoned. She never let
her disability stop her from leading a fully productive,
normal life. She played, attended school, worked,
married, and raised a family. From the time she was a
little girl, she could never understand why her devout
Catholic grandma kept praying for her to be healed.
*Can't she accept the way I am? God made me this way.*

Over the years, Trisha gradually drifted away from
the church and the God who made her. The refusal
of a priest to baptize her first child because she and
her husband weren't members of his church increased
the distance. But eventually, through a series of events
including a divorce, God drew her back home. She felt
loved and accepted in this new church. She was eager to
engage in the community, learn more about God, and
grow in her faith. Her first step was the Alpha course
where participants learned the basics of Christianity:
topics such as who Jesus is, why He died, how to pray,
how to read the Bible, how to be filled with the Spirit,
how to resist evil, and God's healing power today. On
the night they studied healing, her table leader offered to

pray for her to be healed. She refused the prayer. CP was part of her identity. *God made me this way*.

But God kept pursuing her and revealing more of Himself to her and who He created her to be. She took a spiritual gifts inventory and learned she had the gift of faith. She longed to know how He wanted to use her gifting, so her next stop was a women's retreat where she would learn to hear the voice of God. It was perfect timing. On the first day, the leaders had participants pray silently in pairs, instructing them to listen for God's voice to tell them what He wanted their prayer partner to know. When it was time to share what they had heard, Trisha's partner stated boldly, "God is going to heal you." She was stunned. *But God made me this way*. It wasn't what she was expecting to hear. Later on, another word from God confirmed her gifting and her reason for attending the retreat: "God wants you to share your faith." She was elated. This was the word she was hoping and expecting to hear. Now, the question was *how*?

That evening, she went to the front for prayer ministry to ask the question, and she fully expected the Lord to answer. *How do You want me to share my faith, Lord?* As the prayer ministers began to pray, she immediately relaxed. The presence of the Holy Spirit came over her powerfully. *Speak to me, Lord. Speak to me.* Before she knew what was happening, she was flat on her back on the floor overwhelmed by His peace and held captive by His love. Several women knelt around her, praying gently in the Spirit. *I love You, Lord. I could lie in Your presence forever.*

Suddenly heat and tingling spread through all the muscles that had locked her knee in a bent position her entire life. She felt the muscles releasing and extending until her leg was flat on the floor. *Oh Lord, You are so good!* She never asked, but the Lord healed her anyway. He showed her His mighty power to heal and restore. While she was born with CP, and He loved every single thing about her, her identity was not in her disability. Her identity is in Christ alone. His heart's desire for her and for all His children is freedom—forgiveness for the spirit, healing for the body, and deliverance for the soul.

Trisha's faith catapulted to new heights that day. She knows God is real. She knows He is good. She knows He is a personal God. And she knows He heals. Even though her healing isn't fully complete, she is certain that God, who began this good work in her, will continue His work until it is finally finished on the day when Jesus returns (Philippians 1:6). She is confident it will be completed on *this* side of heaven. She is certain He will continue to answer the prayers of her praying grandma. He even gave her a vision to treasure in her heart where she was dancing with Jesus in a field of flowers. But best of all, she now knows what the Lord wants her to do with her gift of faith. She ministers on several prayer teams at her church and prays for people who need a touch from God. She has a special calling to minister to those who want prayer for physical healing. She loves to share her faith and tell them about Jehovah-Rapha, the God who heals.

# Amazing Faith

*When Jesus heard this, he was amazed. Turning to those*
*who were following him, he said, "I tell you the truth,*
*I haven't seen faith like this in all Israel!"*
Matthew 8:10

When Jeff was diagnosed with prostate cancer, he wanted to keep it to himself. He didn't tell his neighbors, and he didn't tell his coworkers. He asked his wife not to tell the extended family, either. For him, his cancer was a private matter. He didn't want people talking about him or pitying him. Especially not pity. He had surgery to remove the prostate, and the doctor wanted to monitor his PSA closely to determine if there were still cancer cells in his body requiring further treatment. All was well until the checkups. He hated the checkups. The fear was paralyzing. His wife finally convinced him to attend a cancer prayer and support group at the church they attended. He finally agreed, but it was a big stretch for him. Religion was also a private matter, and his prayer life had always been between him and God. He couldn't imagine letting perfect strangers close enough to pray for him.

Unlike Jeff, a Roman officer in Capernaum had a different approach. He let nothing stand in the way of asking Jesus for help. When his valuable servant was sick and near death, he believed that Jesus had the power and authority to heal. Even though Roman soldiers were hated by the Jews, he came humbly before Jesus, pleading, "Lord, my young servant lies in bed, paralyzed and in terrible pain." When the Lord offered to go to his home and heal the servant, the officer said, "Lord, I am not worthy to have You come into my home. Just say the word from where You are, and my servant will be healed. I know this because I am under the authority of my superior officers, and I have authority over my soldiers. I only need to say, 'Go,' and they go, or 'Come,' and they come. And if I say to my slaves, 'Do this,' they do it." Jesus was amazed. This hated Gentile had faith that put the Jewish leaders to shame, and many like him would experience the Kingdom of heaven while those for whom the Kingdom was prepared would miss out. "I haven't seen faith like this in all Israel!" He exclaimed. Then Jesus said to him, "Go back home. Because you believed, it has happened." And the officer's servant was healed that same hour (Matthew 8:5–13).

Many barriers could have kept this officer from asking Jesus to heal his servant. Not only was he a career military man who had authority over one hundred soldiers, but the Romans governed the land and had authority over the Jews. Even so, he set pride aside and showed reverence for their anointed King. He understood Jesus' authority came directly from His Father in heaven. With God Himself granting His authority, the officer had no doubt that Jesus had the power to heal his servant, even from a distance. He didn't let his stature, power, position, pride, or the fact that he was a Gentile stand in the way of seeking Jesus for the help he needed.

Jeff had a spiritual breakthrough when he opened himself up and let other Christians care for him and pray for him. He learned he was never meant to walk through this dark valley alone. When he put his pride and self-sufficiency aside, he experienced the Father's love through the body of Christ for the first time in his life. When they prayed, he had never felt so close to God. He had never felt so worthy of

His love. They pointed him to scriptures that gave him hope. As they discipled him in his faith, God's peace replaced his fear. As he continued to open up, neighbors and coworkers came alongside him to pray and share in his journey. God began to speak to him through people and events that were too impossible to be coincidence. The barriers that had kept him from experiencing the true heart of Jesus his entire life were gone. In spite of his uncertain circumstances, he felt inexplicable joy.

In your own healing journey, be careful not to limit God by your mindsets or religious paradigms. He has the power and authority to heal and restore. He may be waiting for you to put pride, doubt, and self-sufficiency aside. He may be waiting for you to step out of your comfort zone. Let no barrier keep you from receiving the fullness of God's blessing. May He be amazed by your faith!

## Prayer

*Father, Your Word says we are to share each other's burdens (Galatians 6:2), be happy with those who are happy, and weep with those who weep (Romans 12:15). Thank You for Your body of believers, for all those You have put in my path who will come alongside me and walk this journey with me. Through them, I can experience Your love, Your grace, and Your mercy.*

*Lord, I know the enemy wants to isolate me and keep me bound up in old religious mindsets and paradigms. Please reveal any false beliefs that may be standing in the way of my receiving all that You have in store for me. Forgive me when I have allowed my pride, doubt, self-sufficiency, or traditions to stand in the way of experiencing Your power and Your presence. I believe You have the power and authority to heal me. Give me the courage and boldness to break through the barriers that keep me from receiving the fullness of Your blessing. Help me to step out in faith. Give me a faith that amazes You!*

# Wonderful Results

*Confess your sins to each other and pray for each other so that*
*you may be healed. The earnest prayer of a righteous person*
*has great power and produces wonderful results.*
JAMES 5:16

Every Sunday Lindsay heard the pastor invite people to visit the prayer room if they had any prayer needs. She never did. Until today. Today she was desperate. The week before, her doctor called with bad news. The polyps he removed during a routine colonoscopy were malignant. She had more appointments next week to learn about her options. She was terrified. Tossing and turning in her bed the last few nights, she prayed. She begged God for mercy. *Oh God! If it be Your will, please make this all go away! Please, God, don't let me die!*

She was apprehensive when she entered the chapel. She didn't know what to expect. The prayer ministers were kind. They asked questions. And they asked permission to touch her shoulders as they prayed. She felt immediate peace. Then one of the prayer ministers prayed, "Any cancer cells left in this body, I command you to leave now in Jesus' name!" Now she was uncomfortable. *How can you do that? How can you order God to do anything? He is GOD!*

When you receive healing prayer for the first time, it can be helpful to know what to expect. As with Lindsay, the prayer ministers may start by asking you some questions that will help direct their prayers: How can we pray? What do you want God to do for you today? What is the problem or where does it hurt? What was going on in your life when your symptoms first started? Do other members of your family have this condition? Your answers will help them discern if your condition has natural causes or if the root is spiritual. For example, symptoms triggered by a stressful situation could go beyond healing prayer and indicate a need for additional ministry.

When they pray for you, they may use *petition prayers*. Petition prayers are God-directed and show our reverence for His sovereignty and holiness. "Come, Holy Spirit, please bring Your peace into this diagnosis" or "Lord, please forgive me for _____" are examples of petition prayers. Lindsay had deep reverence for God. She humbled herself before Him, petitioning Him to act on her behalf.

It was her reverence for God's sovereignty that led her to question the use of a *command prayer*. This type of prayer is very appropriate when praying for healing. Command prayers are led by the Holy Spirit, directed at the condition rather than God, and prayed with authority in Jesus' name. Jesus and His disciples never used a petition prayer to ask for healing.

The Bible gives examples of command prayers:

- "You deaf and mute spirit…I command you, come out of him and never enter him again" (Mark 9:25 NIV).
- "Standing at her bedside, he rebuked the fever, and it left her" (Luke 4:39).
- "Stand up, pick up your mat, and walk!" (John 5:8).
- "In the name of Jesus Christ the Nazarene, get up and walk!" (Acts 3:6).
- "Be healed!" (Mark 1:41).

Remember, not once in the Bible did Jesus or His apostles pray an "if it be Your will" prayer for healing. Jesus came to save, heal, and deliver—to destroy the works of the devil. And

He left His disciples and all believers with the mandate to "'lay hands on the sick and heal them'" (Mark 16:18). We can pray for healing without adding an "if it be Your will" because we know His heart is to heal.

During Lindsay's prayer time, the prayer ministers were loving and gentle, never preaching, and always attuned to the Holy Spirit. She connected with Jesus, experienced His peace, and felt His love. She left filled with hope, armed with encouraging scriptures, and fully expecting their powerful prayers to produce wonderful results!

## Prayer

*God, thank You that Your will is to heal and restore. Thank You that I can ask You for anything in Your name, and You will do it (John 14:14)! Come, Holy Spirit. Please fill me with Your presence. In the name of Jesus and by His authority, I command this affliction to leave my body and not return. I thank You that I have been healed by Your stripes!*

*Lord, You promise that when two or more are gathered in Your name, You are present (Matthew 18:20). Please lead me to righteous men and women who will come alongside me in my journey and come in agreement with my prayers for total healing. I thank You, Lord, for all You are doing to restore my body to health, even when I can't see it. I trust Your promise that the earnest prayers of the righteous have great power and produce wonderful results.*

# I Declare

*The weapons we fight with are not the weapons of the world. On the contrary, they have divine power to demolish strongholds. We demolish arguments and every pretension that sets itself up against the knowledge of God, and we take captive every thought to make it obedient to Christ.*

2 Corinthians 10:4–5 niv

Josh had quite a scare a few years ago. A blocked artery to his heart almost killed him. Fortunately, he made it to the emergency room just in time. His doctors repaired the blockage with a stent and talked to him about the lifestyle changes he would have to make to cope with his coronary artery disease. For the last five years, he had been diligent. He thanked God for His faithfulness, for rescuing him from the jaws of death. He exercised, lost weight, and made all the dietary changes necessary to keep his cholesterol low. He was compliant with all of his heart medications, and his tests routinely came back within normal range. His latest symptoms were innocuous. A little shortness of breath when climbing the stairs, that subtle feeling that someone was sitting on his chest. He ignored them, until they started to increase and reached the same level of intensity as the first incident. Now, he lay in the cardiac unit waiting for an angiogram. The doctors were convinced it was another blockage. He was devastated.

In your quest for wellness, what do you do when bad news comes or an unexpected turn of events catches you off guard? When your circumstances directly conflict with scripture and what you know and believe in your spirit to be true, you can be tempted to wallow in self-pity, anxiety, confusion, or doubt. Or you can fight for what you know to be true. A powerful and practical way to fight back is through *declarative prayer*. In this type of prayer, instead of making requests of God, you come to Him in prayer and declare His truth. Jesus used scripture in the wilderness to rebuke Satan's lies with the truth of God's Word (Matthew 4:4, 7, 10). Paul gave similar instructions when he said, "Take. . .the sword of the Spirit, which is the word of God" to resist the devil in times of evil (Ephesians 6:17). Declaring scripture over your situation can lift you out of the pit of doubt and change your mindset, transforming you into a new person by changing the way you think (Romans 12:1–2).

Declarative prayer starts by inviting God to access your mind. Pray that He would hold all your thoughts captive, especially those that oppose God's truth, under the authority of Jesus. Then let your thoughts take the form of words that you speak out loud in faith. These words might come directly from scripture or they may be words that God speaks directly to your spirit. Either way, speaking out the promises of God interrupts the reality surrounding you and makes the truth of God's Word personal to your situation. The more you declare what He says to be true, the deeper your roots grow down into Him, and the stronger your faith will grow in His truth (Colossians 2:7).

David gives us a good example of declarative prayer in Psalm 23. In the first verse alone, David doesn't ask God to be his shepherd; he declares that God is. He doesn't ask God to meet his needs; he declares that God will. Throughout the psalm, he declares who God says He is, what he believes God is to him, and what he believes God is doing in his life.

Josh began with scripture that directly related to his circumstances and prayed out loud, making a personal declaration. "I will restore you to health and heal your wounds" became, "You will restore me to health and heal my wounds" (Jeremiah 30:17 NIV). "No weapon turned against you will succeed" became "No weapon turned against me will succeed" (Isaiah 54:17). He countered his symptoms with "You took my infirmities and bore my diseases," and "I am healed by your stripes" (Matthew 8:17; Isaiah 53:4–5 NKJV). Surprisingly, while his medications would need to be adjusted, tests showed no new blockages. The truth of scripture was beginning to manifest in his physical reality.

In your prayer time today, ask God what truth He wants you to know about your circumstances. Wait and listen. Usually the first word or verse that comes to your mind is from God, so don't doubt. Do a word search on Biblegateway.com to locate the specific scriptures and declare them out loud. Let Him shower you with faithful promises and transform your thinking. You have an arsenal of divine weapons at your disposal to beat back the lies of the enemy. Use them!

## Prayer

*Lord, forgive me when I've let the enemy keep me focused on my circumstances instead of the promises of Your Word. I center my thoughts on Your authority, especially those related to my illness. I praise You, Lord! You are the Lord who heals me (Exodus 15:26)! Change my thinking, Lord! Pull me out of this pit of unbelief. Transform my mind with Your truth!*

*Help me to declare Your truth of scripture over my situation, even when no evidence of that truth exists in my physical body. Thank You for sending forth Your Word to heal me (Psalm 107:20). According to Your Word, I believe! Nothing is impossible for You, Lord (Luke 1:37). Thank You for restoring life to my mortal body through the Spirit who dwells in me (Romans 8:11). Thank You for the promise that You will complete the good work You have begun in me (Philippians 1:6).*

# Hidden in the Darkness

*"And I will give you treasures hidden in the darkness—*
*secret riches. I will do this so you may know that I am the LORD,*
*the God of Israel, the one who calls you by name."*
ISAIAH 45:3

Mike, a father of two young boys, battled colon cancer. His doctors were optimistic and his faith was strong. Nearly three years passed. One treatment after another had failed, and one prayer after another seemed to go unanswered. His voice cracking and tears running down his cheeks, Mike said to his pastor, "I can't do this anymore. People pray for me. I cry out to God. Nothing changes. My prayers just bounce off the ceiling. I believe, I really do. *But where is He?"*

Two thousand years earlier, Jesus and His disciples climbed in a boat to cross the Sea of Galilee after a day of ministry. Exhausted, Jesus rested His head on a cushion and fell asleep. While He slept, a fierce storm came up and the high waves began filling the boat with water. Through it all, Jesus slept. Fighting the raging storm, the disciples grew exasperated and finally woke Him by shouting, "Teacher, don't you care that we're going to drown?" (Mark 4:37–38).

Sometimes, it feels like God is sleeping through your storm. Or you may be going through a season like Mike where you can't seem to wake Him at all. You pray and shout, but your storm keeps raging. Your breakthrough doesn't come. You don't even know if God is listening. People keep telling you if you seek Him, you will find Him (Deuteronomy 4:29; Jeremiah 29:13; Matthew 7:7; Hebrews 11:6). Well, you've been seeking. He is silent, hiding somewhere behind a thick veil. You are waiting for Him to break into your darkness, to save the day, to rescue you. You long to stand with Him in victory on the mountaintop, to be a living, breathing testimony of His healing power. But there is nothing. Nothing but silence. Nothing changes. Nothing happens. Nothing moves forward. You can't see Him. You can't feel Him. You can't hear Him. Your cries grow more desperate. You beg Him to show Himself, to prove He is truly awake.

And while you're waiting in the darkness, the enemy is relentless in mounting his attack against you. He convinces you that God really *doesn't* care. He has surely forgotten you (Psalm 44:24). He has turned His face away from you and rejected you (Psalm 88:14). His anger rages against you (Psalm 89:38–48). And now, His silence is the final punishment (Job 13:24). The veil of doubt and unbelief grows thicker.

But God does care. He hasn't forgotten you. And He's not sleeping. He's still right there with you, even though you can't feel His power and His presence. He's hidden in the darkness. *Why would He do that?* Because He may be teaching you not to depend on your experiences—to walk by faith, not by sight. God wants our knowledge of Him to become real and personal. He wants our head knowledge to become heart knowledge. By hiding, He can gently expose our unbelief and teach us to see through the eyes of faith. We learn to trust His ways, even when we don't have a clue what He's doing.

If it feels like God is hiding from you, you might believe the enemy's lies and fall further into the pit of hopelessness. You can cry out to God to show Himself, to break into the darkness and come to you. Or you can go to Him. God may be saying, "Beloved, come to Me. Come up here. Come higher. You want to make sense of your circumstances in your mind and with your emotions. I love you and I am always with you, but I am not speaking to your soul right now. I want to speak to your spirit. I want you to leave the world and all the drama behind and dwell with Me in your spirit. Come up here and I will show you hidden things that you do not know, the deeper things of My heart" (Jeremiah 33:3).

Meeting God in the spirit realm is an act of will on your part. You may have to fight through the lies of the enemy and the darkness of your soul to reach Him there (Matthew 11:12). But if you can surrender your mind and emotions to Him, He can take you to a place where you are no longer moved by your circumstances because you are seeing through the eyes of faith (Philippians 4:11–12); you are seeing through His eyes. You know He is faithful, regardless of the silence, regardless of the storm raging around you. This is the place of true revelation, where He gives you treasures hidden in the darkness, secret riches, so that you may know the One who calls you by name.

## Prayer

*Lord, I cry out to You for healing, but my prayers bounce off the ceiling. Where are You, Lord? Don't You care what this affliction is doing to me? Have You forgotten me? How much longer will You be silent? I'm desperate for Your presence, Lord. The enemy attacks relentlessly, but a thick veil hides You. I can't find You in the darkness. Where are You, Lord? Please don't hide from me (Psalm 27:9)!*

*Help me to fight through this darkness to find You. My heart has heard You say, "Come and talk with Me." And my heart responds, "Lord, I am coming!" (Psalm 27:8). I surrender my mind and emotions to You. Speak to my spirit, Lord. Show me the deeper things of Your heart. Help me to see my circumstances through Your eyes, the eyes of faith. Even when I don't understand Your ways, Lord, I know You are faithful. You give me secret treasures hidden in the darkness.*

# Pit Bull Prayers

*"And so I tell you, keep on asking, and you will receive what you ask for. Keep on seeking, and you will find. Keep on knocking, and the door will be opened to you. For everyone who asks, receives. Everyone who seeks, finds. And to everyone who knocks, the door will be opened."*

LUKE 11:9–10

Ed battled a rare blood disorder. Lying in his hospital bed, he listened as his doctor explained there was nothing more he could do medically. "You need to get your affairs in order," he said gently. Pastors and prayer ministers from his church came. They prayed over him and held prayer vigils. He went through his Bible, pulling out every promise of God that countered what the doctor had said. He wrote the scriptures on sticky notes and tacked them all around his hospital room. He wrote them on note cards and declared them over and over. The doctor still insisted, "You need to get your affairs in order." One by one, the prayer ministers dropped off their watch. Many thought he was in denial. "You need to get your affairs in order," they said. He continued to pray and stand in faith. Only a few remained who stood in agreement with him. Like a pit bull fighting for a piece of steak, he would not let go of God's promises. He prayed fervently. He persisted. In the end, he walked out of the hospital with his affairs untouched. He was healed.

To encourage His disciples to pray and never give up, Jesus told a story of a widow who had the persistence of a pit bull. She had a dispute with an enemy and repeatedly took her request for justice to the judge, who kept ignoring her. This judge neither feared God nor cared about people, but he finally gave her justice because her persistence wore him out. If this unjust judge rendered a just decision, Jesus tells us that God will surely give justice to His chosen people who cry out to Him day and night (Luke 18:1–8). In another passage, He says to imagine you have unexpected company and have to go to a friend's house at midnight to borrow some bread. You find your friend and his family are already settled in for the night, and he tells you to go away. But Jesus said if you keep knocking long enough, he will get up and give you whatever you need because of your shameless persistence (Luke 11:6–8).

How many of us have the faith to pray with such shameless persistence, believing God will eventually answer? Instead, we often pray backwards. We receive before we believe. We pray a few times, asking God for something we need, and if we don't receive it, we give up. Our persistence can be hindered by weariness, unbelief, and doubt that God loves us. But if we believe He truly loves us, we can be confident He hears and answers our cries for help. Jesus made this point clear when He said, "You fathers—if your children ask for a fish, do you give them a snake instead? Or if they ask for an egg, do you give them a scorpion? Of course not! So if you sinful people know how to give good gifts to your children, how much more will your heavenly Father give the Holy Spirit to those who ask him?" (Luke 11:11–13). Even the evil judge relented. How much more will a loving Father respond to your persistent prayers?

Persistent prayer is an expression of your faith that God hears and God answers. It doesn't necessarily mean constant repetition or endless prayer sessions into the wee hours of the night. It does means keeping your requests continually before Him and reminding Him of His promises, just like

Ed did. It means never giving up, even when the answers come slowly. It's knowing that even when nothing appears to be happening, He's working on your behalf because He makes all things work together for your good (Romans 8:28). It's knowing that God is always on your side (Romans 8:31). And it's believing Him when He says that everyone who asks, receives; everyone who seeks, finds; and the door is opened to everyone who knocks. Keep on praying and never give up. Pray with shameless persistence. Pray like a pit bull.

## Prayer

*Father, forgive me when I've given up too soon and allowed my unbelief and doubt to hinder my prayer life. I know You love me, Lord. You hear every prayer, and You always give good gifts to Your children. Help me to keep my eyes fixed on You and Your promises.*

*Lord, help me to keep on asking, keep on seeking, and keep on knocking. Remember Your promises to me, Lord! You are the God who heals, the God who restores! Please give me the faith to persist, to cry out to You day and night for justice when the answers come slowly. Thank You for being my advocate in the courts of heaven (1 John 2:1). Help me to pray without ceasing (1 Thessalonians 5:17 NKJV). Help me to pray like a pit bull!*

## Jehovah-Rapha: Sara's Story

It's every parent's worst nightmare. The phone rings and the voice on the other end says, "There's been an accident." Their thirty-three-year-old daughter, Sara, was working out on a treadmill at the club and had a seizure, causing her to fall and strike her head. They rush to the hospital ICU to be at her side. Two days later, she feels fine and wants desperately to be released. They take her home and stay with her, observing her through the weekend to make sure she has no further complications. An hour after they leave, they receive a desperate phone call. She has a severe, debilitating headache. Upon reaching the hospital where she was rushed by ambulance, the admitting doctor greets them with somber news. *She is close to death*. She needs emergency surgery to relieve the pressure and bleeding on her brain. For five hours, they cry out to God. *Please, God. Please!* Finally, the surgeon comes in and gives them the same somber assessment. *Indeed, she is close to death.* She is in a coma supported by many machines. Her prognosis is guarded to poor. Her path is unknown. They must wait and watch and pray. The journey begins.

They wait and they watch. A multitude joins them in praying for their daughter. Finally, the first miracle occurs. "Sara, can you open your eyes?" asks the nurse. For the first time in four days, she responds to a verbal command. She raises her eyebrows and opens her eyes a tiny bit. *A glimmer of hope!* "We need to control Sara's brain swelling and pressure by keeping her sedated," the doctor explains. "When brain swelling starts to recede, hopefully we can reduce the sedation and see more response." They learn that the C-scan is normal and there is no more bleeding. All other vital signs are normal. Her feeding tube provides the nutrition she needs. She's young. These are all factors in her favor. *Praise God for this good news.* She continues to sleep. They continue to watch and wait.

The next day, a pastor from their church visits and hope rises even more. She bows her head for a few moments and looks up smiling. "I feel God's presence here. Sara is covered in prayer." She points them to Isaiah 41: "Don't be afraid, for I am with you. Don't be discouraged, for I am your God. I will strengthen you and help you. I will hold you up with my victorious right hand" (verse 10). She prays a beautiful prayer over Sara, asking God for a full recovery and little signs along the way. She seems confident in her prayer. They know God is in the midst of their journey.

They continue to watch and wait. For the next ten days, the doctors gradually reduce the sedation. Sara's C-scans are still normal. Visitors continue to come and pray. Little by little, she grows more responsive. A head move. A frown. A cough. She moves her foot and hand. Both arms move. Her eyes open momentarily. *Thank You, Jesus.* Her mom gazes out the wall of windows in her room. Beautiful trees line both sides of the street for many blocks. The sun streams in from early morning until late afternoon. The angle of Sara's bed provides her with the perfect view of the cross on the top of a nearby church. *God is so good. Wake up and see, Sara!*

More watching, more waiting. Mom touches Sara's hand and speaks gently to her. She bats both eyes and looks at her, frightened. Mom comforts her. "You are in

the hospital. You had an accident. You're in a safe place."
She settles down. She knows she is safe. She has surgery
to open a direct airway into her trachea so they can
remove the breathing tube from her mouth. They take
the feeding tube out of her nose and throat and put it
directly into her stomach. She's now breathing partially
on her own. She still hasn't regained consciousness. But
her motor movement is becoming more purposeful.
She's fading in and out, blinking periodically, lifting her
head, frowning, swallowing, and moving and flexing her
arms, legs, feet, and hands. Her doctor is impressed with
her eye movement and ability to obey commands. All
progress. *Praise God!*

Finally, she is off sedation and her brain pressure
is stable. She is awake! She smiles. *Thank You, Jesus!*
Doctors remove the drain to her brain and all the
surgical staples. She continues to improve. As she sits
in a chair facing the beautiful windows, basking in the
sunshine, the neurological team is amazed with her
progress. She follows commands with her eyes open
wide, looking at each person around the room. She still
can't talk because of the trach tube, but she is totally
alert and communicates with expression and eyes. She
scratches and paws at the line of stitches in her head.

Nearly three weeks after the accident, Sara transfers
to another facility for rehab. Again her doctor and the
neurological team are amazed at her progress. A new
trach tube enables her to speak. Mom bundles her up
and takes her outside to enjoy the warm sunshine and
fresh air, marveling that only three weeks ago, doctors
told them their precious Sara was close to death. As the
days in rehab progress, she becomes totally alert and

awake all day. When she removes the trach tube herself, the doctors agree that it's time for her to breathe on her own! Again, Mom marvels at God's faithfulness. On her first day of therapy, she takes seven steps. A week later, she does laps of two hundred steps twice daily. Her first words were a very raspy "I'm hungry," and now she tells the nurse not to wake her up too early and the doctor that she is ready to leave. Her sense of humor is back. She wears her running shoes, walks on her own, and sends text messages to her friends. Her physical strength is returning, and her appetite is ravenous. She attends therapy sessions several times daily. *Praise the Lord for what He has done!*

After three weeks of therapy, she goes to another facility for more intense rehab. Her caregivers call her "the miracle girl." Therapy continues, she showers and grooms on her own, and sleeps and eats well. Nearly two months after the accident, Sara goes home. She continues her therapy on an outpatient basis for a few more weeks. Doctors expect a full recovery. The journey draws to an end, but a new journey begins: the telling of Sara's story, with all glory to Jehovah-Rapha, the God who heals.

# For His Glory

*But when Jesus heard about it he said, "Lazarus's sickness will
not end in death. No, it happened for the glory of God
so that the Son of God will receive glory from this."*

JOHN 11:4

"We must get word to Him," Mary told her sister Martha.
"He will come," she said confidently. The two sisters lived
with their brother Lazarus in Bethany, and he was very sick.
So sick, they knew he would die without the help of Jesus.
Jesus was a good friend, and they had watched Him perform
many healing miracles. Surely He would come, even though
coming back to Judea could be dangerous. The last time He
was in Jerusalem, the religious leaders tried to kill Him. He
fled with His disciples beyond the Jordan to the area of Perea.
"Tell the Lord His dear friend is very sick," she instructed the
messenger. *Surely, He will come.*

She watched and waited. *Surely, He will come. He cares for
us.* She helped Martha comfort their brother. *Surely, He will
come.* But Lazarus was running out of time. With each of
Lazarus's breaths growing more labored, Mary's confidence
went from anxiety to anger, and finally, to devastation. He
didn't come. And Lazarus died.

They prepared his body, wrapped him in grave clothes,
and placed him in the family tomb. They grieved. And all the
while, Mary struggled to understand. *Was it too dangerous?
There must be some reason.* Four days after Lazarus had been
in his grave, they heard from some friends who had come
from Jerusalem to comfort them that Jesus was coming.
"You go meet Him," Mary said to her sister. She waited with

their visitors for her sister to return. *I don't understand. I saw Him heal the sick. Surely, He would have come to save His dear friend.* As her guests consoled her, she looked wistfully out the window, not understanding yet somehow knowing there was an explanation.

Martha was back. Mary jumped up, eager to hear what Jesus told her. Martha called her aside. "I told Him if He had been here, our brother would not have died," she began. "And I told Him that even now, God will give Him whatever He asks for." She hesitated. "Mary, He told me our brother will rise again! He said, 'I am the resurrection and the life. Anyone who believes in me will live, even after dying.' He asked if I believed Him." Martha's face was alive with faith. "I told Him *yes*, I have always believed He is the Messiah, the Son of God!" Then Martha said, "He wants to see you."

Mary left immediately for the outskirts of the village where He was staying. Martha followed behind, along with their guests who assumed by her haste that she was going to Lazarus's grave to weep. When Mary found Jesus, she fell at His feet in anguish and cried out, "Lord, if only You had been here, my brother would not have died." When Jesus saw her weeping and the others wailing with her, a deep anger welled up within Him. And He wept with her. At His request, she led Him to the tomb. The mourners followed, murmuring to each other, "See how much He loved him!" But others said out loud what Mary was secretly wondering. "This man healed a blind man. Couldn't He have kept Lazarus from dying?"

Jesus was still angry when they arrived at the tomb. "Roll the stone aside," He ordered. Martha protested, "Lord, the smell will be terrible!" Unfazed, Jesus said, "Didn't I tell you that you would see God's glory if you believe?" As they rolled the stone aside, He looked up to heaven and prayed, "Father, thank You for hearing Me. You always hear Me, but I said it out loud for the sake of all these people standing here, so that they will believe You sent Me." Then He shouted, "Lazarus, come out!" With her eyes transfixed on the entrance of the cave, Mary was astonished to see her brother emerge, wrapped in grave clothes and very much alive! "Unwrap him and let him go!" Jesus said (John 11:1–44).

In contrast to Martha's confident faith, Mary wondered for all of us. Why does He delay when our needs are so desperate and so obvious? When our time is running out? He waited to come to Lazarus, not because He feared the religious leaders, and not because He was callous and didn't care. On the contrary, He grieved along with Mary, sharing her sorrow and even her anger at death itself. He waited because He knew Lazarus would die, and He would perform an amazing miracle for His glory. Through this miracle, Jesus showed He had power over death, and that even physical death can't take away the life we have in Him. Many believed in Him after this miracle (John 11:45), and it was foundational to the Christian faith—He is indeed the resurrection and the life, and anyone who believes in Him will never die (John 11:25).

When healing doesn't come, and when God doesn't move on your timeline or in the way you expect, He may have a greater purpose. He may be allowing your situation to reach the point of death because He is planning on doing something only He can do, something so powerful and wonderful that it could come only from the hand of God. In times of waiting, you can trust He will *always* meet your needs (Philippians 4:19). Your delay may have a purpose, all for His glory.

# Prayer

*Lord, sometimes I feel like Mary. I know You love me. I know You care for me. I know You know how desperate I am. Lord, time is slipping by and I need You to come now! I don't always understand when the Jesus I know, the Jesus who loves and cares for me, doesn't move in the way I expect. Help me to always trust in Your goodness, Lord, especially in times of delay. Thank You that You will supply all my needs from Your glorious riches given to me in Christ.*

*Lord, You are indeed the resurrection and the life! Thank You that You conquered death once and for all and that in You, I live forever. When I don't understand Your timeline, help me to know You have a greater purpose. Help me to believe and see Your glory.*

# Just Have Faith

*But when Jesus heard what had happened, he said to Jairus,*
*"Don't be afraid. Just have faith, and she will be healed."*
LUKE 8:50

Jairus stood on the shore with a large crowd anxiously watching as the boat came across the lake from Gerasenes. He was a man of stature, the leader of the local synagogue who took care of the building and supervised worship and the rabbis who taught there. It would be out of character for him to do what he was about to do. Jesus was a traveling teacher, and a controversial one at that. But he was desperate, more desperate than he had ever been in his entire life. The boat finally landed, and Jesus and His disciples came ashore. Pushing through the crowd, Jairus fell at Jesus' feet and pleaded fervently. "My little daughter is dying," he cried. "Please come and lay Your hands on her; heal her so she can live!"

Jesus nodded and walked with him, and all the people followed, crowding around Him. While on their way, Jesus stopped suddenly. He turned around in the crowd and asked, "Who touched My robe?" His disciples shrugged it off. "Look at this crowd pressing around You. How can You possibly know who touched You?" But His eyes kept searching the crowd. Clearly, He wasn't moving on until He could see who touched Him. Jairus shuffled his feet impatiently. *Come on, Jesus. We need to keep moving! My little girl is dying!* Finally, a frightened woman came and fell to her knees in front of him. "It was me," she said. "I knew if I could just touch your robe, I would be healed. Immediately, my bleeding stopped, and I could feel in my body that I am healed!" And He said to her,

"Daughter, your faith has made you well. Go in peace. Your suffering is over." Jairus grew more anxious. *Hurry, Jesus. My daughter is suffering!*

Just then, some messengers arrived. "Jairus," they called out. "Your daughter is dead! There's no use troubling the Teacher now." His heart stopped. *It's too late!* But Jesus overheard them and immediately said to Jairus, "Don't be afraid. Just have faith, and she will be healed." Telling the crowd to stay back, He followed an anguished Jairus to his home with only Peter, James, and John at His side. Commotion filled the house when they arrived. They went inside and Jesus asked, "Why all this weeping and wailing? The child isn't dead; she's only asleep." But the crowd just laughed at Him. He told them all to leave and then took Jairus and his wife, along with His three disciples, into the room where their little girl was lying. Jairus's eyes filled with tears when he saw her motionless body. But Jesus took her hand and said, "*Talitha koum*," which means "Little girl, get up!" Immediately, she stood up and walked around! Overwhelmed and totally amazed, Jairus and his wife embraced with tears of joy (Mark 5:21–43; Matthew 9:18–26; Luke 8:40–56).

In this culture, the mourners who wept and wailed over the dead were often paid professionals. These mourners laughed at Jesus. But God made it clear that the world would never know Him through human wisdom, and that our faith might seem crazy and even offend people (1 Corinthians 1:21–22). The enemy will always use the logic of unbelievers and the doubt of skeptics to steal our hope. In the midst of heartbreak, Jesus encouraged Jairus and wouldn't let him give up. Jairus chose to follow Jesus instead of giving in to the scoffing mourners. We have the same choice—either to believe the world or to stand with Jesus and surround ourselves with people who will do the same.

In just one day of ministry, Jesus reached out to a bleeding woman, a demon-possessed man, and a family of the dead—all of whom would have been considered unclean and avoided by the religious leaders of the day. But His compassion changed their lives forever. He feels the same compassion for you. It's never too late to ask Him for help. Your need will never trouble Him. He is never distracted or too busy handling more serious prayers than yours. There is more than enough of Him to go around! Even in His humanity, when He was physically detained by another ministry need, Jesus was able to solve Jairus's problem. He can say yes when the entire world says no because He alone is the source of all hope. And His words to you today are simple. Just have faith.

## Prayer

*Lord, forgive me when I allow the wisdom of this world to distract me from Your presence, Your power, and Your promises. Help me not to focus on the troubles I can see right now but to fix my gaze on the things I can't see. I know these troubles are temporal and will not last, but You and Your promises will last forever (2 Corinthians 1:20). Please bring people into my life who will stand in faith with me.*

*Lord, increase my faith when I'm tempted to give up. Help me to hear Your voice of encouragement above the voices of a world that tries to steal my hope and trample on my faith. Help me to hear Your voice of promise, even when it makes no human sense. Lord, You know my every need and nothing I pray is insignificant to You. No prayer is "too late" to pray. You have the power and the compassion to say yes when the entire world says no. You are my Source of hope. Help me to just have faith.*

# Even Greater Things

*"Very truly I tell you, whoever believes in me will do the*
*works I have been doing, and they will do even greater*
*things than these, because I am going to the Father."*
JOHN 14:12 NIV

"Can I pray for you to be healed?" asked Betty's friend. She sighed. "Sure, you can try. But everyone I know who gets cancer dies from it." "Jesus healed everyone who came to Him," her friend encouraged. "Well, of course He did," Betty retorted. "He was *God*!"

Many like Betty think that Jesus had the power to heal because He was God. It is true that Jesus certainly was fully God. He was sent by the Father (John 5:31–37) to do the works of the Father (John 5:16–18), and He was one with the Father (John 10:30, 38). He is the visible image of the invisible God, He created all things, and He holds all creation together (Colossians 1:15–18). But Jesus was also fully human (Colossians 2:9). His appearance was not particularly special (Isaiah 53:1–3). He hungered, thirsted, and grew fatigued like us (Matthew 4:2; John 4:4–7). He felt emotion like us (John 11:35). And He suffered and died like us, for only as a human being could He die and break the power of sin and death (Hebrews 2:14).

But while He was fully God, Jesus gave up His rights as God and put His deity aside when He walked on the earth (Philippians 2:8). He never used the fact that He was God in the flesh, from the beginning of His ministry when Satan tried to trick Him in the wilderness to the end when He hung dying on a cross. He was the promise of God, sent to bring good news to the poor, release the captives, and free the prisoners (Luke 4:18–21). And He did just that. He made the blind see, the lame walk, the lepers clean, the deaf hear, and the dead rise (Luke 7:20–22). All His power to heal the sick came directly from His Father in heaven (John 10:31–32, 38). Jesus didn't heal the sick as God. God healed the sick through Jesus the *man* (Luke 5:17; Acts 2:22; 10:38).

Just as God healed and performed miracles through Jesus, Jesus healed and performed miracles through His disciples by the power of the Spirit. For example, Stephen, a man full of God's grace and power, performed amazing miracles and signs among the people (Acts 6:8). Philip preached the Gospel in Samaria, cast out many evil spirits, and healed many who had been paralyzed or lame (Acts 8:5–8). In Lydda, Peter instantly healed a man named Aeneas, who had been paralyzed and bedridden for eight years (Acts 9:33–35). Paul and Barnabas performed many healing miracles and wonders in their ministry travels (Acts 15:12; Romans 15:18–19). Paul raised a boy from the dead who fell out a window while listening to him preach (Acts 20:9–12), and he even healed the sick through handkerchiefs that only touched his skin (Acts 19:11–12)!

These men were not God but mere human beings who allowed God's healing power to work through them just like Jesus did when He was here on earth. In the same way that Jesus worked through believers in the early church, He works through us today. In His humanity, Jesus came to show Betty and all of us how to live on the earth as God intended, free from the bondage of sin, intimate with the Father, and working in partnership with Him to advance His Kingdom through the power of His Spirit living inside us. He does His best work through those who are fully submitted and dependent on Him. Today, remember that the same God who placed the stars in the sky and called them by name humbled Himself as a tiny baby. He gave up His rights as God to live in relationship with you. Jesus healed everyone who came to Him. By the power of His Spirit working within you, He can do even greater things.

## Prayer

*Lord, You are no stranger to my suffering. You have felt my pain and You have cried my tears! I will never fully understand the kind of love that would compel You to come to earth as a humble baby and give up Your rights as God. Immanuel, God with us! Thank You for dying a criminal's death on the cross to break the power of sin and death over me.*

*Lord, You came to bring good news to the poor, release the captives, and free the prisoners! You cast out demons and restored sight to the blind. You made the lame walk, the lepers clean, the deaf hear, and the dead rise! By Your authority, the apostles continued to perform signs and wonders in Your holy and precious name. Forgive me when I've doubted Your power and desire to heal today. Thank You that Your Spirit is alive in me and other believers. Lord, You came to show me how to live and walk in that power! Help me to be an obedient vessel, fully submitted to Your will. By Your Spirit within me, You can do even greater things. By Your power, I can be healed.*

# The Secret to Contentment

*I have learned to be content whatever the circumstances. I know what*
*it is to be in need, and I know what it is to have plenty. I have learned*
*the secret of being content in any and every situation, whether*
*well fed or hungry, whether living in plenty or in want.*
PHILIPPIANS 4:11–12 NIV

For three days, the storm raged. He was a prisoner on the way to Rome and tried to warn them of the danger. But they wouldn't listen. Fair Havens was an exposed harbor and a poor place to spend the winter, so the crew wanted to go on to Phoenix. Sure enough, the ship was soon caught up in a wind of hurricane force. They took such a violent battering they were forced to throw the cargo and the ship's tackle overboard. When all hope was lost, he stood up to encourage them by telling of an angel's visit the night before. "I urge you to keep up your courage, because not one of you will be lost; only the ship will be destroyed." *Who is this man? A prisoner who talks to angels?*

On the fourteenth night of the storm, the sailors sensed they were approaching land. Fearing they would smash against the rocks, they dropped their anchors and prayed for daylight. Just before dawn he urged them all to eat in order to survive, and once again he promised, "Not one of you will lose a single hair from his head." *Who is this man that he knows such things?* He took some bread and gave thanks to God, broke it, and began to eat. Once again, they were all encouraged. When daylight came, they could see a bay with a beach and thought they might be able to navigate safely between the rocks to reach the shore. So they cut loose the anchors, lowered the rudders, raised the foresail to the wind, and headed for the beach. But the ship struck a sandbar and the stern stuck fast, the pounding surf breaking it to pieces. Out of options, the commander shouted frantic orders for everyone to jump ship. And just as the prisoner promised, every single person reached land safely.

Upon learning they were on the island of Malta, Publius, the chief official, welcomed them and treated them kindly. When the prisoner learned that Publius's father was ill with fever and dysentery, he prayed for him, laid hands on him, and healed him. Soon, all the other sick people on the island came and he healed them, too. Again the people marveled. *Who is this man?* As a result of his miraculous works, the locals honored the crew and supplied them with everything they needed to set sail again (Acts 27:1–28:10).

The prisoner was the apostle Paul, and he suffered many fiery trials in his service to Christ. In addition to stormy seas and shipwrecks, he faced countless angry mobs that whipped, beat, stoned, and robbed him, bound him in chains, and threw him into prison. He spent many painful and sleepless nights without food, water, or enough clothing to keep him warm (2 Corinthians 11:23–27). As if these circumstances weren't difficult enough, he was afflicted with a thorn in his flesh that some think was a sort of debilitating physical ailment. He asked the Lord to remove it three times, and three times the Lord said no. "My grace is all you need. My power works best in weakness" (2 Corinthians 12:9).

Paul could have given up, but he didn't. He knew the secret to contentment. He could see His life through God's eyes and focus on what God called him to do instead of his own needs and wants. His priorities were aligned with God's. He held on loosely to the things of this world and focused on the eternal. He knew he could do nothing apart from Christ (John 15:5). He performed many extraordinary miracles in spite of his ailment because he learned to depend on God's power, not his own. In Christ, he could do all things (Philippians 4:13).

Paul encouraged and ministered to the sick and hurting, even as a shipwrecked prisoner. He wanted everyone to know the Source of his comfort and hope, and that even in the direst circumstances, God is more than enough. As the storm rages around you and your ship appears to be sinking, you can trust He will give you everything you need—courage to face every challenge, grace to overcome weakness, confidence to trust in His provision, obedience to bless others, and a heart that aligns with His. In Him, you have found the secret to contentment.

## Prayer

*Father, I am weak. The storm has raged for too long, and I feel beaten down and shipwrecked. Thank You that in this place of weakness Your power will carry me! Help me to depend on Your strength instead of my own. In You, I can do all things!*

*Lord, when I desire more, please help me be content with what I have. Help me to be content in every circumstance and to know and trust that You will supply all my needs (Philippians 4:19). In this time of waiting, You alone are the Source of my comfort and hope. You are more than enough. I need Your courage, Lord. I need Your grace. Break my heart for what breaks Yours. Help me see through Your eyes and bless others as You have blessed me. You know everything I need, Lord. You know the desires of my heart. But I need You more. You alone are the secret to my contentment.*

# I Am

*"I am the LORD who heals you."*
EXODUS 15:26

You've prayed and you've been patient. But wellness doesn't come, at least not in the way you expect or on your timetable. Your hope rises and you are convinced your breakthrough is coming, only to find it delayed, or even set back by an unexpected turn of events. The same questions go through your mind over and over again. What are You doing, God? What do You want from me? What am I missing? Please hurry, Lord! Time is running out!

When healing tarries, always remember God has perfect timing. He has not forgotten you. He has many ways to heal, and as we have learned, His methods and timing are not always predictable. Sometimes Jesus healed through a touch or a word and sometimes from a distance. Sometimes He waited. Sometimes He healed in front of everyone and other times He insisted on privacy. Often His methods made no sense at all, like mud on the eyes, spittle on the tongue, or bathing in a pool. It's never up to us to decide how or when, but however healing comes, He controls it all. He is the One who heals our diseases (Psalm 103:3). He can heal by physicians, surgeons, climate, renewed mindsets, common sense, a direct touch of the Holy Spirit, and much more.

God provides physicians to prescribe medications to destroy mutated cells, kill harmful organisms, and regulate body systems. He gifts surgeons with the ability to remove unwanted tissues and repair defective organs. He uses sunny, dry weather to bring health to the bones of the stiff and crippled. He uses counselors and ministers of inner healing and deliverance to help us heal from wrong mindsets and the wounds of our past that can have a significant impact on our physical health. Through forgiveness and the release of bitterness, God can rewire old toxic thought processes, causing the body, soul, and spirit to be healed and restored. He also gives us common sense and a sound mind to make good choices. God has established natural laws for health and wellness. Our health can improve greatly when we avoid harmful addictive behaviors, exercise regularly, eat the foods we were created to eat, and take care of our bodies.

Sometimes He bypasses all of His natural methods and heals instantly through a direct touch from the Holy Spirit. If we're honest, we would all love to be healed miraculously and instantaneously. But often, healing is a process, a process God always uses for good. During the healing process, it can feel as though time stands still. Discouragement gives way to hopelessness, and you feel so mentally, physically, and spiritually weary that you can't go on. At times like this, remember Jesus will never leave you or forsake you (Hebrews 13:5). He keeps track of your sorrows and has collected every precious tear in a bottle (Psalm 56:8). He has personally felt your pain and will not waste a single tear. He promises to make all things work together for your good (Romans 8:28).

Dear one, this is the time to seek God like never before. Pray like the persistent widow who never gave up until her request was granted (Luke 18:1–8). When you can't pray another prayer, take comfort in knowing that the Holy Spirit prays for you with groaning that cannot be expressed in words, and the Father who knows your heart knows exactly what the Spirit is saying (Romans 8:26–27). Surround yourself with people who will pray for you, encourage you, lift you up, and help you keep your eyes on Jesus. Keep worshipping Him, being confident that the Lord Himself inhabits your praises (Psalm 22:3). Stand on His Word, and constantly remind Him of His healing promises until your faith displaces all your doubt and fear (1 Corinthians 16:13). Turn your worries into prayers, telling God what you need and thanking Him for all He has done until you receive His promised peace that surpasses your ability to understand (Philippians 4:6–7). Comfort and bless others in their troubles as He has comforted you (2 Corinthians 1:4). Release all bitterness and forgive your enemies so that nothing can stand between you and your God (Matthew 5:23–25).

If you can persevere during this sacred healing process, God promises that you will reach a place of maturity and completeness where you will lack nothing (James 1:4). In this place of deep intimacy, you find He is enough. He is all you need. He is the great "I Am" (Exodus 3:14). "I Am love, peace, joy, provision, kindness, goodness, hope, grace, and faithfulness. I Am all you need. I Am the God who heals you."

## Prayer

*God, thank You for Your perfect timing and for all the ways You heal and restore. Help me to trust You when I can't go another day. Help me to press in to You like never before. Thank You for the gift of prayer and worship. Thank You for Your Word and Your promises! Help me to be grateful when healing tarries and to bless others in the midst of my own sorrows. Help me to forgive those who have wounded and betrayed me.*

*Lord, You are enough. You are all I need. I want You, Lord. Your unfailing love is better than life itself (Psalm 63:3)! The one thing I seek most is to live in Your presence all the days of my life (Psalm 27:4). Lord, I want to be healed, but I want You more. In You, I am complete. In You, I lack nothing. You are Jehovah-Rapha. In You, I am healed.*

## Jehovah-Rapha: Your Story

*"Arise, my darling, my beautiful one, come with me."*
Song of Solomon 2:10 niv

In your quiet time today, close your eyes and imagine. You are walking along the deserted seashore at dawn. Gazing across the blue water, you see distant hills barely visible through the morning mist. As you make your way along the rocky shore, you notice Someone standing on the beach at a distance. He waves at you and motions you to come. You can't resist. It looks like He's tending a fire as wisps of smoke intermingle with His long white garment blowing in the gentle breeze. As you get closer, you smell something good. Your stomach immediately reminds you how long it's been since you've last eaten. You arrive at His campsite, and you see He has a meal waiting for you—fish cooking over a charcoal fire and some bread.

"Come and have some breakfast!" He says with a broad smile. You don't dare ask Him, "Who are you?" Somehow, you already know. It is the Lord. He motions for you to sit and serves you the bread and the fish. You eat a delicious meal together in silence. When you are finished, He says to you, "Walk with Me." You're walking in silence along the beach when He stops, reaches down, and scoops up a handful of sand. Letting it run through His fingers, He says, "My thoughts about you far outnumber the grains of sand on all of My seashores" (Psalm 139:17–18). You ponder those words for a moment as your gaze shifts to the water. He continues, "My love for you stretches out as far as you can see. It's wide enough to cover the sorrows of today and long enough to cover your uncertain tomorrows. It reaches up as high as the heavens are above the water and as deep as the ocean floor. It touches the heights of your good times and the depths of your despair [Ephesians 3:17–19]. Nothing can keep my love away from you [Romans 8:38–39].

You can barely take in His words when He says, "Come with Me." You suddenly find yourself in another place (Revelation 4:2). A door stands open before you. You look down and realize you are wearing a radiant white robe. He smiles and says, "You can freely enter because you wear the garment of salvation, My royal robe of righteousness [Isaiah 61:10]. You are made clean by My blood." Gratefulness floods your heart (Philippians 4:6). All your doubts are immediately gone.

He takes your hand and leads you through the door. You enter a magnificent room, filled as far as your eyes can see with worshippers, all dressed in beautiful robes like yours. The sights and sounds overwhelm your senses. The music is unlike anything you have ever heard. Your knees crumble underneath you, but He holds you steady. Suddenly the crowd parts and forms a long, wide aisle to the front of the room. You look down at the shiny glass floor, sparkling like crystal, leading to the throne. And then you see Him. He is as brilliant as the finest gemstones and an emerald glow circles His throne like a rainbow. He beckons you to come.

"Are you ready?" He asks gently. You nod, barely able to breathe. He raises His right hand slightly and faces the throne. Your hand rests on His as He escorts you down the aisle where Abba Father waits (Galatians

4:6). As you get closer, you notice several others in white robes seated on thrones around Him, all wearing gold crowns. You approach Him, and the light grows more and more intense. You immediately drop to your knees before Him, not daring to look up. But the Lord assures you, "You are worthy. Lift up your head and seek His face. Receive His blessing" (Psalm 24:5–7). Then He takes His place at the Father's right hand (Mark 16:19).

Obediently, you open your eyes and lift your head. You behold His glory. Wave after wave, His love overpowers you. His splendor is like the sunrise. Rays of light flash from His hands where His awesome power is hidden (Habakkuk 3:4). You have waited your entire life for this moment. The deepest longings of your heart are fulfilled. Joy overflows. He completes you. He is enough. But you know He has more. You say, "Abba, though I walk in the midst of trouble, You will revive me. You will stretch out Your hand against the wrath of my enemies, and Your right hand will save me" (Psalm 138:7 NKJV). He reaches out His right hand and you feel His power pulsate through you, instantly restoring you to full health.

"Holy, holy, holy is the Lord God Almighty, who was, and is, and is to come," shouts all of heaven in one voice (Revelation 4:8 NIV). You join in their joyous celebration: "Lord, You are the Lover of my soul, the Lifter of my head. Words cannot express my gratitude for all You have done for me. I was unclean and You made me righteous. I was broken and You made me whole. You comforted my broken heart and gave me beauty for ashes, joy instead of mourning, and a double portion in my land instead of shame and dishonor

[Isaiah 61:1, 3, 7]. I cried to You for help, and You restored my health. You brought me up from the grave, Lord. You kept me from falling into the pit of death [Psalm 30:8–9]."

"Beloved child, come up here," Abba Father gently coaxes. You find yourself sinking into the very lap of love itself, your heart beating as one with His. "Abba, what great love You have lavished on me that I should be called Your child! [1 John 3:1]. I delight in You, Lord. In You, my heart is pure, my hands are clean, and my mind is filled with the truth of Your love, although it is far too great for me to fully understand. My soul rejoices! To You who is able to do exceedingly abundantly more than all I can ask or imagine, according to Your power that is at work in me, to You be the glory forever and ever [Ephesians 3:20–21]! To You, Jehovah-Rapha, the God who heals!"

# About the Author

Mary J. Nelson is an author, speaker, and associate pastor (non-staff) of Prayer and Freedom Ministries at Hosanna! Church, a church of seven thousand members in Minneapolis–St. Paul, Minnesota. She was the founder and president of Soterion, a communications company dedicated to the healthcare industry. Mary has a passion for helping people encounter God and His goodness in the midst of trials and be empowered and set free to live out their destiny. She emerged from a breast cancer diagnosis in 1999 eager to share how God restored and transformed her life. Her deepest desire is to give away what she has freely received.

Mary is the author of *Grace for Each Hour: Through the Breast Cancer Journey* (Bethany House, 2005), *Hope for Tough Times* (Revell, 2009), and *Peace for Each Hour* (Comfort Publishing, 2013). Her books inspire those suffering from physical, emotional, relational, and spiritual brokenness by helping them draw close to the heart of God. She founded and leads the Pray for the Cure cancer healing and discipleship ministry at Hosanna! where she also serves as a leader in the Sozo inner healing ministry and healing prayer ministry. She and her husband, Howie, have two adult children and two grandchildren and have been married for thirty-nine years.